THE WORLD OF
MINIATURES

First published 2018 by
Guild of Master Craftsman Publications Ltd
Castle Place, 166 High Street, Lewes,
East Sussex BN7 1XU, UK

Reprinted 2020

ISBN 978 1 78494 402 5

A catalogue record for this book is available from the British Library.

Publisher: Jonathan Bailey
Production: Jim Bulley and Jo Pallett
Consultant Editor: Sarah Walkley
Senior Project Editor: Wendy McAngus
Editor: Judith Chamberlain
Managing Art Editor: Gilda Pacitti
Designer: Chloë Alexander

Colour origination by GMC Reprographics
Printed and bound in China

THE WORLD OF
MINIATURES
FROM SIMPLE CABINS TO ORNATE PALACES

CONTENTS

PLANNING

THE IMPETUS FOR A MINIATURE project may come from anywhere. For some miniaturists an interest in a particular style or period dictates the design of property they create, while for others it may be a film, a holiday location or even a single piece of furniture picked up at a dolls' house fair. Those making shops often talk about having spent so much time trying to perfect a single type of miniature (be it cakes or kitchen appliances) that they find they have amassed quite a collection – one that can only realistically be displayed in a shop setting.

My own house is a copy of a Georgian townhouse set in the Edwardian period. Choosing to model a house at the dawn of the 20th century allowed me to include many 'modern' inventions from electric light to the telephone and gramophone, but was also the way I got round other restrictions. When I first started collecting dolls' house furniture in the early 1980s, the vast majority of what was available was either Victorian or Georgian. One of the first items I bought was a cast-iron kitchen range. I could not imagine a house where there was a range in the kitchen, but more modern fixtures and fittings in other rooms, so I decided to make it an Edwardian setting.

That does not mean that the house is devoid of modern elements. It has many features that were not possible when I started collecting, such as remote-controlled lights, a ringing doorbell, flickering fires and smoking chimneys.

OPPOSITE With tiled walls, marble pillars and intricate painting around the filigree arches, this box room could easily take up residence in the Alhambra.
Maker: Ron Hubble

This is just one area of the hobby that has developed. The materials and techniques are changing from a time when collectable items tended to be made largely in wood to ones cast in white metal or resin and, now increasingly, 3D printed.

The range of house styles being modelled has expanded significantly with modernist houses and contemporary cottages joining the ranks of Victorian and Edwardian properties. There is no longer a restriction to stop at houses either. Over the coming chapters, you will find garden sheds, lighthouses and witches' lairs to name but a few of the different properties that miniaturists are now modelling.

The book sets out to inspire you about the various different alternatives. Each chapter focuses on a style of building, starting with the grand Georgian and Victorian mansions but then looking at more modern homes, coastal properties and fantasy locations. It showcases the work of many talented miniaturists and finds out where they get their ideas.

The presentation of the various properties is interspersed with pages giving you advice on how to make everything from the basic core of your dolls' house to the finishing touches like rugs and food to put on the table.

Whether you are embarking on a new project, or trying to solve a technical challenge with an existing one, I hope this book provides you with the inspiration you are looking for.

SOURCES OF INSPIRATION

ABOVE Intrigued by Japanese culture, Peggy Connolly decided to make her own *Ryokan*, or inn. The 1:20 scale kit was released in instalments with a magazine by DeAgostini Italy. It took nearly two years to collect all the parts.
Maker: Peggy Connolly

RIGHT The Liberty Chesham Cabinet House takes a Colonial Indian Almirah (a type of cabinet sold by Liberty's in the 1900s) and archive fabrics to create a modern take on the cabinet houses that inspired the dolls' house hobby.
Maker: Emma Mawston

ABOVE Two very British-styled Doll's House Emporium kits were combined to create Varykino, the summer dacha from Boris Pasternak's love story *Dr Zhivago*. The house is a cosy, but rather dated, Russian country house, giving Jo Medvenics hours of fun making things look neglected and overgrown.
Maker: Jo Medvenics

ABOVE This 1:12 scale room box entitled *Psyche opening the door into Cupid's garden* replicates the pre-Raphaelite painting of the same name by J. W. Waterhouse.
Maker: Josje Veenenbos

RIGHT A stripped-back palette has been used to create this fantasy house. Inspired by old movies, Tom Roberts created a series of monochrome rooms; accents of silver and gold have been added for a touch of Hollywood glamour and opulence.
Maker: Tom Roberts

ABOVE Artist Jessica Townsend Melton has combined her love of working in glass with a fascination for all things miniature to create a world entirely from glass. The pieces in the house reflect the style of furniture in her childhood home, while bricks and wallpaper designs are sandblasted on to the walls.
Maker: Jessica Townsend Melton

Styles of 'building'

Wealthy families used to have specific rooms to show off their dolls' houses. But with space at a premium, today's miniaturists need to adopt more space-saving approaches.

HISTORICALLY, MINIATURES WERE always displayed in a small house or multi-roomed cabinet. The houses contained a full suite of rooms fulfilling different functions and decorated in a consistent way. Many modern miniaturists still follow this format, creating a scaled-down house in the style and period of their choice. But other forms of display are becoming just as popular because they are considered more practical and offer greater flexibility.

The early houses were owned by aristocratic families as a way to show off their wealth and give girls experience of household management. These families typically had space to display a miniature house in its own room, which is a luxury that few modern miniaturists have.

RIGHT AND OPPOSITE
This five-storey house had so many rooms, it was decided that it would make a perfect hotel.
Maker: Emma Waddell

BELOW Fascinated by the story of consummate craftswoman Mary Delany, Christine Bloxham made this room box to explore some of the same techniques in miniature.
Maker: Christine Bloxham

Space dictates the style of house for many modellers. A dolls' house which opens at the front and the back has to be placed in the middle of the room to be accessible from all sides. Half-depth houses that open at the front only are increasingly popular in Europe as they can then be pushed against the wall. In the USA, where domestic properties tend to be larger, dolls' houses open at the back and are still displayed in the centre of the room.

Room boxes are small display units that are designed to hold a single scene. Their small size means that they can be accommodated on a sideboard or bookshelf, making them ideal for modellers who are short on space. Window boxes are smaller still. They are of a limited depth, providing room to display only a small vignette or diorama, but tend to be small and light enough to hang on the wall.

Room and window boxes have a number of advantages over multi-room houses. Room boxes can be built to any scale. As a result, they are a relatively cheap way for a miniaturist used to working in 1:12 scale to experiment with working in 1:24 or 1:48 scale.

'The early houses were owned by aristocratic families as a way to show off their wealth.'

They are quicker and easier to complete. The maker only has to focus on building the one room. When building and decorating a dolls' house, it is important to spend time planning the construction; lights in one room have to be installed before the floor is laid in the room above. This degree of planning is not necessary for an isolated room box.

Room boxes also offer the possibility to experiment with a range of different styles. It is possible to create a Victorian kitchen scene in one box and a 21st-century café in another. Many miniaturists like the degree of flexibility that room boxes afford.

Room boxes do still need thought and planning. The most successful scenes incorporate false walls and doors, hinting at a world beyond. The display also needs a clear focus, otherwise it can easily appear as a collection of objects in a small space.

Many miniaturists make a combination of both houses and room boxes. They have their 'main' house and then create room boxes when they have an idea for a specific scene, or want to try their hand at modelling in a different scale or period.

HOUSE STYLES

ABOVE A multi-storey house can take up a lot of room, but it gives the miniaturist scope to model a full suite of rooms. This house has been decorated in the Regency style, inspired by a documentary about Byron's London house, 13 Piccadilly Terrace.
Maker: Tee Bylo

RIGHT AND FAR RIGHT Modelling a whole house gives scope for all sorts of ageing and weathering. Americans Pat and Noel Thomas created this property in the 1980s at the time of the Mount St Helens volcanic eruption. The volcanic ash that fell was put to good use to create a dusty porch.
Maker: Pat and Noel Thomas

ABOVE The interior of any dolls' house does not necessarily have to be of the same period as the exterior. This Tudor house has been 'renovated' so that it suits the needs of a modern miniature family.
Maker: Susan Stobart

ROOM BOXES

RIGHT In his short story, *The Library of Babel*, Jorge Luis Borges describes a vast library of interconnecting hexagonal rooms that houses all possible books of a certain format and style. Working in 1:7 scale, artist Charles Matton has created a room box which hints at a greater library beyond.
Maker: Charles Matton

BELOW At the other end of the scale, Carol Black has had a vast cabinet built to house her collection of miniatures. The cabinet allowed her to accommodate many more rooms than would be the case in a traditional house and at 19½in (500mm) deep, each room box is also larger.
Maker: Carol Black

Questions of scale

Before embarking on your dolls' house project it is important to decide which scale you would prefer to work in, depending on the space you have and how many items you plan to make from scratch.

MINIATURES COME IN A WIDE RANGE OF standard sizes from 1:144 or micro-scale at the lowest end of the range up to 1:6 for some large architectural models. Before embarking on any dolls' house project, it is important to decide which scale you are going to work in. It is possible to combine different scales as Joelle Sheard-Patrick shows in furnishing her 1:16 scale house with 1:12 scale items (see page 80), but this is very tricky to get right.

The key issues to consider are the room you have available to display your miniatures and how confident you feel about creating items from scratch; a 1:48 scale house will take up a lot less room in your house, but you may have to scour the internet for furnishings as fewer makers tend to work in this scale.

The most widely adopted scale is 1:12 or one-inch scale. It was used for Queen Mary's Dolls' House when it was built in the 1920s and subsequently became the *de facto* standard because it is large enough to allow for the creation of highly detailed miniatures. However, even a relatively modest cottage can stand 26in (660mm) high and take up a floor space of 18¼ x 18¼in (460 x 460mm). With the

LEFT AND FAR RIGHT
Inside this model of Beacon Hill there is an even smaller version on the landing, showing that it is sometimes possible to work in two scales at once.
Maker: Jennifer Kennedy Halter

exception of a few children's toys such as Sylvanian Families (Calico Critters), it is not commonly used by other modelling hobbies, e.g. model railways, meaning that there is limited opportunity to buy some accessories like animals for a 1:12 scale farm.

For both these reasons, 1:24 scale (half scale) is gaining ground. Buildings are half the size of 1:12 scale houses, so modelling a row of shops becomes a more feasible proposition; there is no need to give over most of a room to a street scene. It is also the scale used for garden, or G Scale model railways and die-cast cars, making sourcing animals, figures and vehicles easier. It is not favoured by many dolls' house artisans because of the challenges of creating detailed models in this scale, but with the advent of computer-controlled laser cutters, many suppliers of dolls' house kits are making their furniture ranges available in 1:24 scale.

The big area of overlap between dolls' house and railway modelling is in 1:48 scale, also known as quarter scale. In the US, it is the ratio used for O Gauge railways; in the UK and Europe the ratio is slightly smaller, but sufficiently similar that 1:48 scale buildings do not look out of place. Railway modellers have adopted new techniques such as 3D printing and laser cutting more quickly than dolls' house makers. As a result, there are a lot of 3D printing files and kits

ABOVE A lot of makers work in 1:12 scale because it allows you to achieve a phenomenal level of detail, as is clear from this stunning drawing room.
Maker: Ann Taylor

available that can be adapted for use by the dolls' house modeller working in 1:48 scale.

The smallest scale is 1:144, or micro-scale. This is similar to N Gauge in railways, but is also one-twelfth of anything built in 1:12 scale. As a result, dolls' house artisans are beginning to produce items in this size that can be displayed on their own or as a dolls' house within a dolls' house.

1:12 AND 1:24 SCALE

LEFT AND BELOW
Having worked predominantly in 1:24 or 1:25 scale as a set designer, Terry Brown moved up to 1:12 to make this house, inspired by the work of Scottish architect Charles Rennie Mackintosh. The interior draws on elements from real Mackintosh properties including Hill House and the architect's home 120 Mains Street in Glasgow.
Maker: Terry Brown

ABOVE When experienced miniaturist Jean Nisbett saw this 1:24 scale cottage, it reminded her of a Dorset cottage she used to spend holidays in – so she just had to buy it. She has furnished it with flagstone floors and an Aga, just like the real one.
Maker: Jean Nisbett

SMALLER SCALES

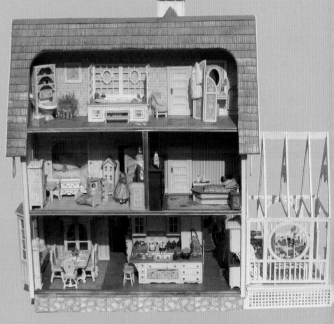

ABOVE AND RIGHT When Heather Drinkwater first began the 1:48 scale Pickett Hill, modelling in such a small scale was in its infancy. In fact, she was something of a guinea pig. Many of the furniture kits that she used had only just been released when she bought them.
Maker: Heather Drinkwater

BELOW Nell Corkin specialises in 1:144 scale miniatures. This exquisite country cottage could be a dolls' house within a standard 1:12 scale dolls' house.
Maker: Nell Corkin

FOUNDATIONS

BUILDING A DOLLS' HOUSE IS A FUN and rewarding process. It gives you the opportunity to truly make it yours and customize every aspect of the building. Whatever the style or period of the property, there are a few basic principles that you need to observe. Following these guidelines will make the whole process easier and, ultimately, more enjoyable.

Successful construction starts with planning. Certain aspects of the construction and decoration need to be completed before others can begin. For example, wires from ceiling lights are typically threaded through a hole in the ceiling and then run across the floor of the room above, so you do not want to install the flooring on the first floor until the ceiling lights are in place in the ground floor rooms.

As a result, it is critical to contain your urge to complete whatever construction tasks seem most appealing at the time and think about the order of construction. The accomplished miniaturists featured in this book all note how they start by sketching what they have in mind and then translating that into detailed lists of what needs to be built in what order. Do not worry if you are not good at drawing; the sketches are for your reference only so no one else needs to see them.

To help with your planning, the technique and advice pages throughout the book highlight where completion of one task is dependent on another.

OPPOSITE Trained in building conservation, Richard Wilson is trying to translate everything he has learnt in the real world into his miniature construction.
Maker: Richard Wilson

Complete as much of the construction, painting and finishing of components as possible before final installation. It is always much easier to work on a flat workbench than on a vertical surface or in a tight space. For this reason, lay flooring on a thin piece of wood or card then slot it into the house, or paint doors, architrave and skirting before gluing in place.

If you need multiple versions of a feature – for example several windows of the same size – there is no need to make each individually; make one and use that as the master from which to mould the rest. It is far less time consuming and the results are much more consistent.

Increasingly, miniaturists are designing components on computer and then 3D printing them. This has the added bonus that the computer file can be printed in any scale, so there is no longer a need to make a new master if you move from modelling in 1:12 scale to building in 1:24 scale.

Spend time just looking and imagining. Look at real houses, books and home-style magazines and trawl the internet. This is great way to get inspiration and to check key stylistic details, whether it is a precise colour palette or an authentic historical feature.

Never be shy about asking other miniaturists for advice. Most miniaturists are happy to share how they would go about a particular task. Many are also active bloggers and have written about their experiences in their blogs.

Assembling a kit

Many newcomers to the dolls' house hobby will prefer to buy a ready-made house and concentrate on the decoration and furnishing. If you have decided to take on the challenge of constructing your own house from a kit, here are some practical tips to supplement the instructions provided by the manufacturer.

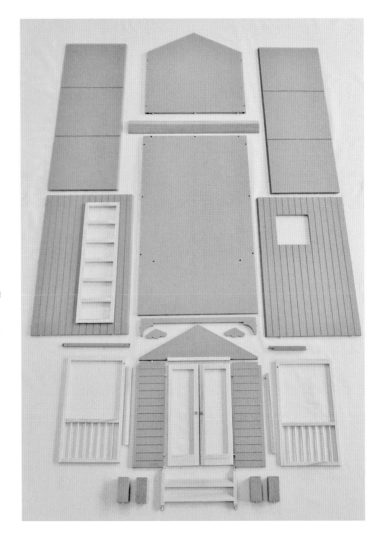

1 First check that all the parts are included in the kit. Lay them out and familiarize yourself with each piece.

2 Carefully read the instructions provided, checking which parts are needed at each stage of assembly and making sure that you understand how they fit together.

3 Sand each piece until it is smooth using fine sandpaper, grade G or 00.

4 Check that any pre-cut grooves are the right size to accommodate adjoining parts and that they slot together easily, but securely. You may need to make minute adjustments by sanding to ensure a perfect fit.

5 Assemble each stage 'dry' and check all is correct before you glue any parts together. Once the glue has set it will be difficult to undo without damaging your kit. This is also the stage to plan the order of the decoration. It is easier to rout out grooves in wall and floor panels for lights before they are glued in position.

6 Paint the exterior walls. It is much easier to apply textured or stencilled brick finishes working on a flat panel and without any windows or sills in the way.

7 Paint the ceilings, so that you do not have to do this working upside down when the house is assembled. If you are going to have the same colour ceilings throughout, you can paint the entire panel in one go, but be careful not to allow too much paint to get into the grooves where the partition walls slot in. Even a thin coat of paint may mean that the house does not slot together easily any longer. If you intend to have different coloured ceilings in each room, dry assemble the house and turn it upside down, then you do not have to work against gravity when painting. For smaller properties with only one or two rooms, such as beach huts and cabins, it may also be possible to paint the interior walls.

TOP AND RIGHT Lay out the kit to familiarize yourself with the pieces, then dry assemble them to make sure you know how they fit together.

8 Glue the house together in the order recommended in the manufacturer's instructions.

9 Ensure that walls and floors are at right angles, or you could end up with a leaning house. Check every angle with a set square and if necessary improvise a jig using blocks of wood with perfectly squared corners, a stack of Lego bricks or even piles of books. Use the jig to support the structure while the glue dries. At this stage, it is also best to hold the pieces firmly together with masking tape, as it will be several hours before the glue has fully gone off.

10 If a staircase is provided, but is not designed to be installed during the initial assembly, it is far more practical not to glue it in place until you have decorated the rooms. If it does have to be installed as part of the construction process, be sure to varnish or paint it as much as possible before gluing it into place.

RIGHT This house is now built and ready for decoration.

Building from scratch

Most people new to the dolls' house hobby start by building a kit. However, if you have a particular style of property in mind then you may struggle to find a kit that is suitable. One option would be to commission a professional dolls' house builder to make the carcass for you – though this can be costly; the other is to build the house from scratch.

PLANNING YOUR HOUSE

Start by creating a plan of what you are trying to achieve. Some miniaturists use 3D interior design software, but most just work with pencil and paper to sketch the rough design and then more accurate scale drawings. These are used to work out the exact measurements of each component part and the materials needed.

Dolls' house plans are freely available online. Even if they are not the right style, it is worth spending time looking at them to understand how other modellers draw their plans. Typically you will need a drawing of each side, or elevation, of the house, indicating where the doors and windows will go. You will also need a floorplan for each level of the house, indicating the size and position of individual rooms. You may want to make drawings of specific details that might be more difficult to make, such as a porch or dormer window. That way you can be sure that you have visualized how they will look from every angle. When drawing the floorplans, remember to allow for the thickness of the sheet material that will be used for the interior walls, typically at least ⅛in (3mm); the board used for exterior construction is thicker, typically ¹⁵⁄₆₄in (6mm).

MATERIALS

Dolls' houses are usually cut from plywood or medium density fibreboard (MDF). Some modellers work with model board or foam board; this is really only suitable for smaller constructions and may not take the weight of a large multi-storey dolls' house. It is useful for making a rough initial model of a project, if you find it easier to visualize certain parts of the project in 3D.

MDF is a manufactured material created from hardwood and softwood fibres compacted with resin. It is generally very easy to work with, but produces a lot of dust when cut. It also provides a good, neutral surface for later decoration. Many commercial dolls' house kits are made of MDF.

Plywood is made from thin veneers of wood, with the grain alternating in direction between layers to create strength and minimize shrinkage, warping or cracking from exposure to heat or humidity. When cutting, the outer layers have a tendency to splinter, so care needs to be taken when making openings for doors and windows. Buy the best quality plywood that you can afford; more expensive plywood has more layers and a closer grain, so the likelihood of splintering is reduced.

CUTTING AND JOINING

Whichever material you choose, you need to start by cutting out the panels for the exterior walls. Once cut, the edges should be sanded to a smooth finish. A small block plane is ideal. You will need to ensure that the panels are clamped and well supported, so that the edges remain square. You then want to dry assemble the panels to form a box and ensure you have a good fit; do not glue them at this stage.

BELOW A block plane is useful for sanding the edges.

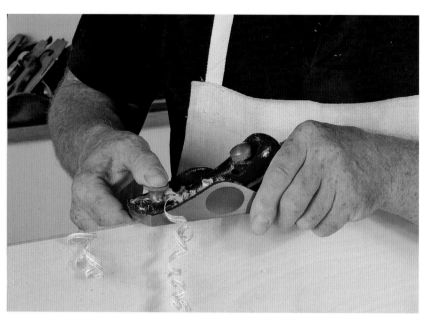

ABOVE An edge-to-edge joint is usually strong enough.

LEFT Always dry assemble the house before gluing.

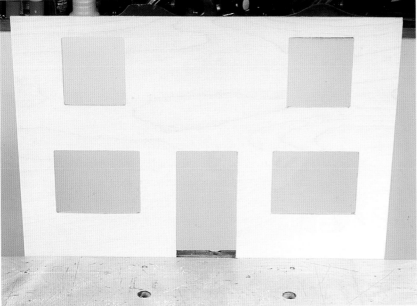

ABOVE Once you have cut the panels to the right size, cut out the doors and windows.

LEFT Coving can be used to create a bracket for the floor divider to sit on.

There are many methods that can be used for joining the panels together. The most basic is a butt joint, or edge-to-edge joint. The sheet material for dolls' houses is relatively light and comes under little load, so this is usually sufficient. It is critical though that the edges are straight as the two sides are only in contact over the relatively thin width of $^{15}\!/_{64}$in (6mm).

You could use small pegs or dowels to strengthen the join. The pegs are inserted into holes drilled into the side of one panel and into corresponding holes on the face of the adjoining panel.

The strongest way to join the boards is to use mortise and tenon joints, cutting a square cavity (mortise) in the face of one panel to receive the tenon tongues cut into the sides of the other piece.

Whichever joining method you use, you now need to deconstruct your house to mark and cut the openings for the doors and windows. The box is then reassembled (still as a dry construction) so that you can measure and cut the room dividers. In a relatively simple dolls' house, you are likely to have a consistent size and shape of room on all floors. This means you can have partition walls that go from the ground floor to the attic. Only cut the holes for the internal doors once you have checked the partitions are a good fit, then mark and cut grooves in the partition walls at ceiling height into which the floor for the upper storeys can be slid.

If you are not confident using a router, consider attaching coving to the partition walls and using this as a 'shelf' on which the floor can sit. The disadvantage of this approach is that you cannot later use the coving as a way to conceal any rough edges of wallpaper.

Now, with your core walls and partitions in place, you are ready to begin decoration. Only glue the whole assembly together once you have completed as much of the decoration as you possibly can.

Exterior finishes

Much of the time, a dolls' house sits closed up on its stand or a shelf, so that the exterior is on display far more than the detailed rooms inside. Getting the exterior right is important to ensure that the house always shows its 'best side'. Depending on the finish you want, there are many approaches that you can take to decorating the outside.

PAINT

The most common solution is to paint a dolls' house. You may need to start by applying a layer of primer. This is critical for plywood houses, but is also a good idea for those made of MDF, which is quite absorbent and otherwise soaks up a lot of paint. To give your house a textured appearance, you can use a masonry paint, such as Sandtex, or add sand to standard emulsion. Specialist dolls' house 'builders' merchants' also sell finishing powders that you mix with paint to create a stone-like texture.

When painting, do not worry too much about plain emulsion going on to areas that are going to be painted another colour later. However, do remove any traces of textured paint as soon as possible, preferably before it dries. If you leave the textured paint to dry it will have to be sanded off before another colour can be added, especially if the affected surface is meant to have a smooth finish, such as a window frame. Any roughness on the frame will be quite visible later.

You could also consider 'rendering' your house, by applying a thin layer of filler to the external walls with a glue spreader. You can vary the texture by stippling the filler as it begins to dry. For a flaky effect, dab the filler with a sponge or add texture using a toothbrush. Practise first on a spare piece of wood to achieve the desired effect. Once the filler is dry, you can paint it in your chosen colour.

STONE AND BRICK FINISHES

There are a number of ways to achieve a brick finish. Perhaps the easiest and least time consuming is to apply brick paper to the outside of the house. These look quite good from a distance, but lack depth.

LEFT This house has been rendered and painted to give it an authentic Parisian feel.
Maker: Linda Corswell

Individual brick slips offer a more realistic alternative, particularly as they are often made of genuine brick. They give you the varied mix of colours that would be expected from a brick wall. But applying brick slips is a slow process. It can also end up being prohibitively expensive for large areas.

Brick slips are stuck to the exterior using tacky glue. Working from the bottom of the wall, you build them up in rows, alternating between a full and a half brick at the start of each row to get the staggered look of a brick wall. You will need to leave a gap of ³⁄₆₄in (1mm) between bricks so that you can apply grout once the glue is dry.

Several dolls' house suppliers make brick stencils in different patterns from English bond bricks to rough stone. The exterior walls need to be painted a cement colour before stencilling. The base colour will be visible between the 'bricks' after the finish has been applied, giving the appearance of mortar. The stencil is temporarily stuck to the exterior using spray adhesive. You then make up a brick compound which is applied in thin layers over the stencil. When the compound is dry, peeling the stencil away reveals raised areas where the holes in the stencil were. The compound is usually brick or stone coloured, so looks quite effective as it is. However, a final touch up with acrylic paint will add depth.

ABOVE LEFT AND RIGHT A brick pattern can be created by scoring bricks into the wood then painting.

BELOW For an authentic brick finish, it is more effective to add blocks of colours.

A final option is to score lines into the walls to indicate the shape of bricks and then to paint the exterior. This technique is most effective on hardwoods and heavily compacted materials like MDF. Composite materials like plywood tend to splinter when scored. The grooves may also close up when painted, with the result that the definition is lost.

After an initial coat of a plain brick red colour, you will need to apply successive layers of yellows, reds and purples to build up variation in the tone of the brick. The temptation is to dot around randomly, painting each brick a different shade. However, it is more effective to work in blocks. When constructing a real house, builders lay successive batches of bricks. All the bricks in a batch will have been manufactured at the same time and will be relatively similar in shade. A final wash of cement-coloured paint simulates mortar. This should be very thin, so it flows into the grooves and does not stick to the brick-coloured surfaces.

CLAPBOARD

American houses and many coastal properties tend to be made of wood, or at the very least faced in clapboards. These are long thin planks of wood that cover the outside in an overlapping pattern. They are easily made using thin strips of plywood, or again can be imitated by scoring lines into the exterior walls.

Roofing

Applying individual tiles to the roof of a house is the crowning glory of a project. For true realism you can invest in real terracotta or slate, but this may be prohibitively expensive. A cheaper option is to make your own. Whatever the material, individual tiles need to be laid following the same method.

1 Make sure the surface on which the tiles are to be stuck is clean and dry.

2 Glue a thin ⁵⁄₆₄in (2mm) strip of card or wood across the lower edge of your roof; this will allow the first row of tiles to lay at the correct angle.

3 To help keep your rows level draw a pencil line across the roof where your first row of tiles will start. The first line is ²⁵⁄₃₂in (20mm) from the bottom edge, including the width of the ⁵⁄₆₄in (2mm) strip. Continue to draw lines all the way up the roof remembering to allow each row of tiles to overlap by approximately half the height of the tile, e.g. if your tile is ⁵⁵⁄₆₄in (22mm) tall, you will need to allow about ²⁵⁄₆₄–⁷⁄₁₆in (10-11mm) between each pencil line.

4 Start on a straight piece of the roof, not one interrupted by dormer windows or chimney breasts. Spread some tacky glue along the bottom edge of the roof and begin to lay the first row of tiles. You will need to cut the final tile to fit; they never fit perfectly, so you will always have to cut the end one. Most tiles can be cut easily by scoring a cut line and using a craft knife, pincers or tile pliers to cut along the line. Odd-shaped pieces can be achieved by sanding with medium-grade sandpaper.

5 For the next course spread glue on the top edge of the tiles that have already been laid and up to the next line drawn. Start laying the tiles for the next row so that the top of the tile is on the next line and the tile is inset by half a tile's width; this will give you the overlapping effect of a real roof. Cut a tile in half widthways to use for the start of the row. Keep the other half for another row further up.

6 Repeat until the roof is covered on both sides. If you are going to add ridge tiles later, work all the way to the top of the roof, cutting the last line of tiles horizontally so that they line up with the top edge.

7 Once you have finished tiling your roof, glue the ridge tiles into position, so that they cover the edges of the main tiles where they meet at the apex. Allow approximately ³⁄₆₄in (1mm) between ridge tiles, if you intend to grout them in (see Tiled floors, pages 66–67). Leave to dry.

TIP: If you alternate between sides of the roof when laying the tiles, it gives the previous course time to dry.

LEFT Lay tiles in rows working from the eaves to the apex of the roof.

ALTERNATIVE ROOFING MATERIALS

Dolls' house makers are remarkably creative in coming up with alternative ways to create roof tiles. Here are a few you might like to consider.

WOOD STRIPS

Strips of wood can be laid in rows across the house. Cut strips 1in (25mm) wide from ¹⁄₁₆in (1.5mm) thick plywood sheet pre-painted to your chosen roof colour. Draw lines across each strip to mark out individual tiles 1in (25mm) wide. Score along these lines but only for three-quarters of each marker; each row covers the unscored area of the strip below.

WOOD TILES

Cut squares 1 x 1in (25 x 25mm) from ¹⁄₁₆in (1.5mm) thick plywood sheet pre-painted to your chosen roof colour. You will need to ensure that you also paint the tile edges, as these will be visible on the final roof.

CARDBOARD SQUARES

The cheapest way to make imitation tiles for a dolls' house is to cut cardboard squares from cereal packets pre-painted to your chosen roof colour. It is also possible to buy precision-cut card tiles. This has the advantage that they are all exactly the same size.

LABELS

Price tag labels with a curved end and a hole for the string double as an effective alternative to slate; you will need to paint them an appropriate shade of grey. These can be used either way up; the scalloped ends make a very effective ridge tile, or decorative detail within a plain design.

ABOVE Cardboard squares make an effective alternative for terracotta tiles.

PRINTED PAPERS

Printed sheets are generally the least expensive option for covering a roof. However, these lack the three-dimensional effect of other options. Use individual tiles if you have the patience; they look much better than paper and are easier to work around awkward shapes.

3D ROOF TILE SHEET

Often made of MDF, these are pre-cut and scored to look like tiles, giving a reasonable 3D effect. They come in a wide range of colours and styles and are ideal for a big plain stretch of roof, but can be difficult to cut around dormer windows and chimneys.

TIP: Paint the roof tiles before you cut them from the sheet; that way you can randomize the pattern on the tile and they are all individual rather than uniform.

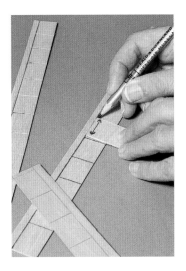

LEFT Wood strips are a quick way to cover a roof.

RIGHT Price tag labels with a curved end can be used to make an attractive pattern.

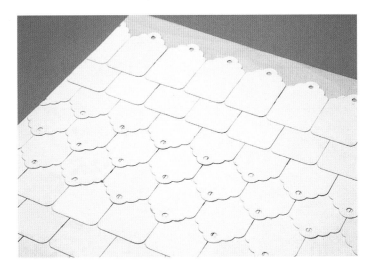

Windows and doors

Doors are available both ready-made and in kit form in a number of different styles. However, it is easy to make your own if you want doors of a particular style and size.

MAKING A DOOR

1 Place a piece of card – an old cereal packet or greetings card will do – behind the door opening and hold it firmly in position with a book or piece of wood. Draw round the opening and then cut out the card template. You will want to repeat this for each door that you are making, because your door openings are unlikely to be exactly the same size or entirely square in every room.

2 Use the template to cut a wooden door from plywood. If the walls of your house are about ¹⁵⁄₆₄in (6mm) thick, then plywood of about ⅛in (3mm) thick is ideal. If your walls are a little thicker – up to ²³⁄₆₄in (9mm) thick – then it looks better if you make your doors from ⁵⁄₃₂in (4mm) thick plywood. Use the best quality plywood that you can afford. Cheap plywood has a tendency to rough up when scored and cut, making decoration difficult.

3 Try your basic door for size, sanding down where necessary until it fits the doorway with a slight clearance all round. If you have yet to fit the flooring, leave a little more of a gap at the bottom to allow for the floor covering. If you are going to use pin hinges, you will have to allow for a bottom step.

4 Now decorate your door. For a simple country-style door, gouge vertical grooves (use a metal ruler to ensure straight lines) in the plywood to simulate planks. If you do not have a sharp gouge, use a fine screwdriver instead.

Alternatively, glue beading to both sides to form rectangular panels or panel them using the same technique as for wall panelling (see page 55). Unless you intend to paint the door, it is best to stain each of the component parts before gluing them on to the base door. Sand the edges of your decorated door and recheck that it still fits your doorway.

LEFT Make a template by drawing around the door opening.

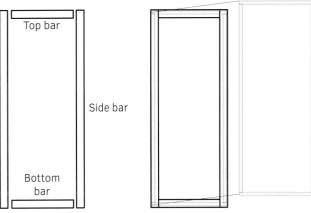

ABOVE Fitting a hinge.

HINGES

If your room dividers have not yet been glued into the house carcass then hinging a door is a lot easier. However, if they are fixed in place, then the choice of hinging is limited. For example, you will find it impossible to inset brass hinges if you cannot work on the walls flat. In dolls' house construction, the most commonly used type of hinge is a pin hinge.

This method uses steel dressmaker's pins to make pin hinges.

1 Drill a fine hole in the top edge of the door as close to the corner as possible and make a corresponding hole in the door frame.

2 Press the pin into the door as far as it will go. Cut off the head and reverse the pin so you can poke the sharp point hard into the hole in the frame.

3 Insert another pin into the bottom edge of the door and cut off the head.

4 You will now have to make a doorstep that sits between the open frame to take the other end of the pin.

TIP: If when you have hung your door it does not swing freely on its pivots, sand the hinge edge to make it slightly rounded.

WINDOWS

Ready-made windows are available in most sizes and styles, but you can easily make your own. You will need to know the size of the aperture and the thickness of your walls. Dolls' house windows are made from strip wood. The finished size needs to be the same thickness as the walls, usually $^{15}/_{64}$–$^{9}/_{32}$in (6–7mm).

1 Measure and cut two uprights the height of your window out of $^{5}/_{64}$ x $^{13}/_{64}$in (2 x 5mm) strip wood and a top and a bottom bar that are the width of your window less $^{25}/_{64}$in (10mm) (the width of the uprights). Glue them together to form a rectangle.

2 Cut two strips from $^{5}/_{64}$ x $^{5}/_{64}$in (2 x 2mm) strip wood that are the full width of the window and two uprights that are the height of the window less $^{5}/_{32}$in (4mm). Glue them together to form a rectangle.

ABOVE Make one frame from plywood (*above left*), then make a second frame from narrower plywood (*above*). This will sit on the first frame and create a lip for the glass to sit inside.

3 Glue the two rectangles one on top of the other. You will now have a frame with a lip to take the window glass.

4 Cut a middle glazing bar from $^{5}/_{64}$ x $^{5}/_{64}$in (2 x 2mm) strip wood that is the internal width of the frame and two uprights that fit between the middle bar and the top and the middle bar and the bottom. Glue in place.

5 Paint the entire frame before fitting the window glass.

TIP: Glaze windows with clear acetate rather than actual glass because a reflection on the window looks more authentic. Acrylic or polycarbonate sheet is tougher, but is prone to scratching.

Stairs

In many dolls' houses, stairs are relegated to a secondary role, tucked at the back or the side of the property. It is not uncommon to find miniature stairs leading nowhere, or ending abruptly where they meet the hall ceiling. In many cases, this is due to a lack of space. However, if you are aiming to make your property as realistic as possible, then including stairs that serve all floors is essential.

PLANNING AND DESIGNING

The key to all aspects of the dolls' house hobby is careful planning, but nowhere is this more important than when it comes to constructing a staircase. If you are building a house from scratch, then the room layout has to be organized around the stairs. If the stairs run up the middle of the house, then you will be constrained to having a room on either side of the stair well; if they go up one side of the house – as in a British terrace or semi-detached house – then all the rooms will be on the opposite side. This may also limit where you install windows, as you would not want the steps to run across the opening; instead the window should be at a height from which someone on the stairs could look out.

When designing the layout, you also need to think about whether you will incorporate any landings. A long, straight run of stairs could easily need to be the full depth of the house to ascend the height from one floor to the next. A landing halfway up a run of stairs allows you to change direction and contain the space the stairs take up. If space really is at a premium, then a spiral staircase may be the answer.

The most difficult part is often working out the height and depth of each step. In 1:12 scale, each stair rises by about ⅝in (16mm). To calculate the number of stairs you need, you have to divide the distance between the floor level on one floor and that on the storey above by ⅝in (16mm). So if the height between two floors is 12¹⁹⁄₃₂in (320mm), then you would have 20 steps. You may have to adjust the height of the steps slightly, e.g. using a ¹⁹⁄₃₂ or ⁴³⁄₆₄in (15 or 17mm) rise, to end up with an exact number of steps.

Each tread is usually ¾in (19mm) deep. Multiplying this depth by the number of steps you have will give you the overall depth of a straight staircase. This will indicate whether you need to add a landing to fit the staircase into the space available. On a spiral staircase, treads are typically the same depth at the outside edge, but much narrower in the middle to create the turn.

The last of a run of steps is the floor level of the floor above, so in the above example you would only need to make 19 treads. However, unless you are having open-backed stairs, you will need to cut 20 pieces of wood to form the backs of these stairs. The back pieces typically sit on top of one tread, but under the tread above. As a result, when calculating the size of each back piece, you will need to allow for

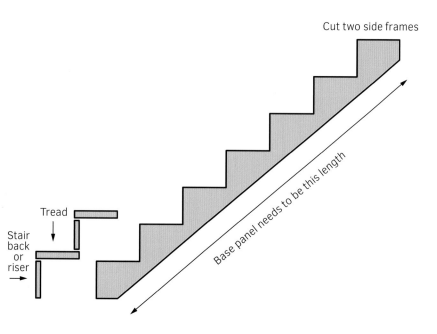

Cut two side frames

Tread

Stair back or riser

Base panel needs to be this length

the thickness of the wood being used for both the tread above and below. If you have a ⅝in (16mm) rise and are using a ⅛in (3mm) sheet to make the stairs, each back piece will need to be ⅜in (10mm) tall.

CONSTRUCTION

Stairs are constructed on a base frame. For a straight staircase, you will need to cut two strips of wood that will form the sides of the stairs. They are cut in a zigzag fashion; each 'tooth' has to be cut to reflect the height and depth of the steps. The side pieces are mounted in parallel on a piece of board that is the width of the staircase and the diagonal length from the base of the stairs to the edge of the top step. The framework for a staircase with a landing is made up of several smaller frameworks, one for each flight.

Stairs should never be fitted until they have been painted, finished and carpeted, as they are very tricky to do *in situ*. You may want to do some of the interior decoration before you fit the stairs, e.g. laying the hall floor or wallpapering a side wall. If you do decide to lay the flooring, remember to take its depth into account when you calculate the necessary rise for each step.

You should also fit as many of the balusters to the staircase as possible before installation. It may be necessary to add the last few after installation simply because, if they were fitted, the stair construction would not pass through the hole in the floor above. However, it is best to keep the number of balusters that have to be added later to a minimum.

Balusters typically go up the side of the stairs and round the landing at the top to prevent anyone from falling down the stairs. They should all be the same height, typically around 2⁶¹⁄₆₄in (75mm) long. For a straight staircase, this should mean that a straight banister rail sits neatly on top, but on some more elaborate staircases, the rail may need to curve as it reaches the top.

RIGHT A set of stairs winding up through the house makes a truly impressive focal point.
Maker: Ann Taylor

GRAND ESTATES

AMONG THE BEST KNOWN AND MOST iconic dolls' houses are properties such as Queen Mary's Dolls' House on display in the UK, the scale model of the White House at the Presidential Hall of Fame and the exceptional models in the KSB Miniatures and Thorne Rooms collections. Most of these represent grand houses and palaces of the like few of us could ever hope to inhabit, which is why so many choose to model them in miniature. It is the ultimate form of wish fulfilment, building the dream house that we could not otherwise afford.

A palatial style dolls' house is an opportunity to collect and display some of the impressive and beautifully crafted artisan miniatures that are available, from miniature silverware to elaborate furniture reflecting the work of craftsmen such as Chippendale and Sheraton.

Unless you have an unlimited budget, you need to be selective about the pieces you buy. Judiciously combining artisan-made miniatures with cheaper mass-produced items and homemade accessories will create the 'wow' factor. As in a real house, there are signature pieces and more workaday items.

The important thing is to think about where the money would have been spent in a real palace or stately home to impress visitors, and install your statement pieces in those rooms. Reception rooms, such as the drawing room, dining room and library, would have been designed to receive guests and so tend to be more

OPPOSITE A replica of Ham House in Richmond, UK, this property was meticulously recreated from plans, photographs and site visits. The original Ham House stood at the heart of fashionable Stuart court life and was filled with the most luxurious and sophisticated items taste, craftsmanship and money could create. The miniature is no different, with gilded barley-sugar columns, floors inlaid with exotic woods and hand-painted ceilings. *Makers: Kevin Mulvaney and Susie Rogers*

elaborate. A few well-chosen artisan pieces can really help lift these rooms. In the kitchen and the servants' bedrooms, practicality was more important, so these can be furnished with more basic, everyday items.

Spend time looking at pictures of real houses and visiting stately homes to see how they are furnished. Unlike some of the properties featured in later chapters, which replicate contemporary or childhood homes, few of us have an immediate sphere of reference and need to seek inspiration from elsewhere to be able to furnish a grand house convincingly.

Unless you particularly want to, you do not have to 'stick to the rules' religiously and furnish the house with items solely from one period. The great palaces and houses of Europe were all added to and adapted by successive owners. They would have modernized and replaced some furniture, but kept hold of precious family heirlooms from previous periods.

Finally, as Annemarie Kwikkel demonstrates, it is not necessary to have a massive dolls' house to enjoy a little slice of luxury. You would never know that her rococo parlour is anything other than a room in a Viennese palace; there is certainly nothing to suggest that it is a self-contained 1:12 scale room box. She also demonstrates that it is possible to upscale quite cheap items by re-upholstering them in silk and adding a touch of gilding. Again this is a great way to reserve your budget for the statement pieces that really catch the eye.

PALACES AND STATELY HOMES

ABOVE This entrance hall features a spectacular double staircase with views of statues in the reception room beyond.
Maker: Nevile Wilkinson

BELOW Few houses have the space to create a ballroom such as this with its porticoed doors and double height ceiling.
Maker: Liza Antrim

RIGHT Set in around 1810–20, the English Rotunda and Library epitomizes the Regency period, with its classically inspired columns, pilasters and busts.
Maker: The Thorne Rooms

LEFT The Restoration Drawing Room shows the decorative nature of panelling, ceilings and furniture which developed during the 'Restoration' of the monarchy from 1660. The intricate carving on both the panelling and the furniture reveals the influence of the skilled Huguenot craftsmen that fled to the UK from France in this period.

Maker: John Hodgson/Hever Castle

ABOVE The figures here have been made in several pieces to allow them to move and be automated. Hinging the cellist's arms was particularly difficult as he needs to be able to move from both the shoulder and the elbow.

Maker: Gale Bantock

LEFT Real silk has been used to line the walls of this music room. The harpsichord, which features a reproduction of Constable's *The Hay Wain*, is one of Ann Taylor's favourite pieces.

Maker: Ann Taylor

LEFT After a flood forced him to rebuild his room box scene, Robert Off decided to build something 'elegant, rich in tradition, vague as to time frame and an environment befitting a successful gentleman of the sea'. The result is the Captain's Table – a dining room hung with naval themed paintings.
Maker: Robert Off

ABOVE Jacky Miles had to ask her husband Leon to make the dining table specially, as she could not find one long enough to accommodate 10 guests for dinner and her impressive collection of miniature silverware.
Maker: Jacky Miles

LEFT This elaborate desk contains everything required to keep up-to-date with correspondence.
Maker: Liza Antrim

ABOVE The floor of this dining room features a complicated parquet design. Having drawn out what he was trying to achieve, the maker kept putting it off, knowing how difficult it would be and how much work it would take. However, in the end it is the feature of Dewell Manor that evokes the most pride.
Maker: Giac Dell'accio

RIGHT Inspired by the great English country houses including Chatsworth, Boughton and Burghley, Giac Dell'accio made this bedroom fit for an earl.
Maker: Giac Dell'accio

RIGHT Ann Taylor painted her own wallpaper to ensure the room had the bold Chinese style that she was looking for. She painted some beading gold that she found in a model railway shop and used this to cover the joins in the corners; this gives the impression that the walls are lined with silk.
Maker: Ann Taylor

Wood flooring

Until the advent of wall-to-wall carpet in the 20th century, wood was the predominant material used in flooring, as it was both relatively warm and durable. Getting the style of flooring right can really add to the period feel of a room. Early floors from the 15th and 16th century were made of simple planks in timbers like oak, ash and elm. More elaborate styles developed in the 19th century first in the grand houses of the day and then in domestic properties. Block and herringbone parquetry came to the fore in the Victorian and Edwardian eras as advances in tools and manufacturing techniques made it possible to create regularly sized blocks.

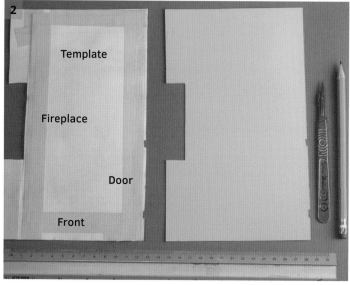

MEASURING THE FLOOR

1 Cut a paper template to the dimensions of your floor. This method requires no measuring. Cut small pieces of paper to fit in all the interior corners, and cut strips of paper to go along the edges of the walls, fireplaces and doors. These should overlap the corner pieces. Tape all the joins together; if the template does not fit well add extra pieces of paper. Add a final piece of paper to cover the 'hole' in the middle. Turn the template over and add more tape if necessary to hold it together. It does not matter what it looks like as long as it is accurate.

2 Make any helpful notes on the template to ensure it is the correct way up. Place the template on a piece of card and draw around it with a sharp pencil; a neutral colour would be better than the yellow card that has been used here for clarity. Cut out the card and check that it is a good fit for the room. Here the indent fits around a chimney breast. This is the basis on which you can lay any of the following types of wood flooring. It is also useful for fitting carpets and tiles.

MAKING PLANKED FLOORING

1 Apply good quality double-sided tape to the underside side of some wood veneer. Press the tape firmly into the grain of the wood. A wallpaper roller is useful to get an even application. If you are using sheets of veneer that are wider than the final floorboards, apply masking tape to the top of the veneer and press down well again. The masking tape will help to prevent the veneer splitting and make marking out easier and clearer.

2 Decide on the width of the planks (usually between 19/32–1in (15–25mm), depending on the size of the room). Mark out the strips with a pencil and a metal ruler. A sharp craft knife is essential; make an initial light cut and then increase the pressure. Give the metal ruler and the knife tip a light rub with some candle wax to help them glide more easily.

3 Remove the masking tape and the tape backing and apply the planks to the card. Firmly press down to ensure the adhesive grips. Cutting the planks to random lengths and laying them end to end gives the impression of floorboards.

4 Wrap medium-grade sandpaper around a block and sand along the grain, being extra careful at the edges. When the veneer is smooth, change to a fine-grade sandpaper.

5 Apply your chosen finish (varnish, lacquer, shellac or wax polish). It is also possible to stain or paint the floor at this stage, if you want a slightly different colour.

6 Turn the floor over and trim away any excess using the edge of the card as a guide. Take extra care at the ends by knifing from the corners towards the middle to prevent the veneer splitting. Finally, check to ensure it fits in the room. Carefully sand any edges that are too tight. The floor can be fixed with glue, sticky wax or double-sided tape.

TIP: Specialist woodworking centres sell rolls of veneer edging, which is narrower and avoids the need to cut strips. Some veneer edgings have adhesive backing and are applied to the base by ironing.

TIP: Polish and finish wooden floors before cutting and putting them into the house; it makes for a cleaner finish.

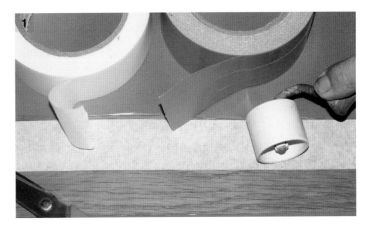

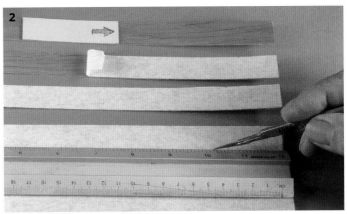

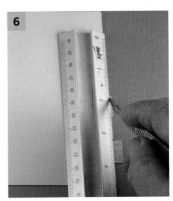

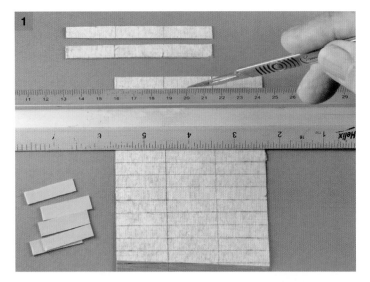

MAKING PARQUETRY SQUARES

1 Follow the first stage of making planked flooring by taping the veneer on both sides. Mark out strips that are 1⅛in (28.5mm) long and then divide them into pieces that are ⁹⁄₃₂in (7mm) wide. When four of the ⁹⁄₃₂in (7mm) strips are placed edge-to-edge, this will give a square that is 1⅛ x 1⅛in (28.5 x 28.5mm). A small card template ⁹⁄₃₂ x 1⅛in (7 x 28.5mm) makes marking out easier. Cut the long strips. When measuring out, take care to mark the pieces so that the grain runs along the 1⅛in (28.5mm) length.

2 Use strong scissors (kitchen shears) to cut the strips to length. This is easier than cutting with a craft knife. Cutting along the grain with scissors is not advisable.

3 Peel off the tape backing and apply four strips in one direction followed by four strips at right angles. Firmly press the blocks down as you progress and the remove the masking tape. Should you have any wide gaps, fill them with a darker shade of filler before sanding. Sand and finish as for the planked flooring.

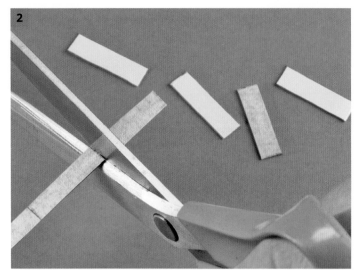

MAKING HERRINGBONE PARQUETRY BLOCKS

1 Draw a vertical line down the centre of your floor template and then add lines at 45° to act as a guide. Follow the first two stages of making parquetry squares, accurately marking out blocks 1⁷⁄₆₄ x ²⁵⁄₆₄in (28 x 10mm). Cut the pieces as for the parquetry squares.

2 Apply a centre column of blocks and then work rows back and forth in the direction of the arrows (picture 1). Sand and finish as for the planked flooring.

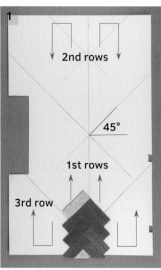

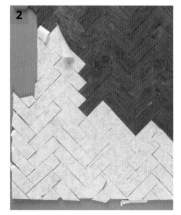

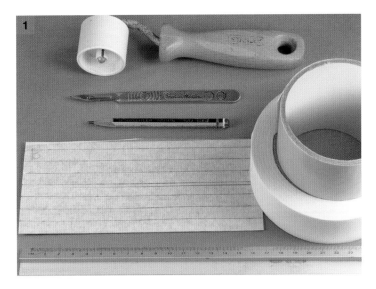

MAKING PERSPECTIVE CUBE PARQUETRY

1 Prepare three different veneers with tape as described in the first stage of making planked flooring. Mark out each one into ²⁵⁄₆₄in (10mm) wide strips.

2 Place a ruler along the bottom edge of the veneer, then rest a 60° set square on the ruler. Draw a line near the centre of the veneer. Measure ²⁵⁄₆₄in (10mm) intervals each side of the 60° centre line and at 90° to it. Continue drawing the 60° lines – a sharp pencil and accuracy are important at this stage.

3 Accurately cut the ²⁵⁄₆₄in (10mm) strips. It is a good idea to mark the strips as once they are cut, the colours can look remarkably similar.

4 Strong scissors will cut the diamond shapes. Draw a vertical line ²⁵⁄₃₂in (20mm) in from the edge of the card and start to apply the repeat pattern. Press the veneers down with a roller. If the diamond shapes vary a little they can be checked for fit before the backing paper is removed. Trim the half shapes along the edges when the pattern is complete by turning the floor over and using the card backing as a guide. Sand and finish as for the planked flooring.

TIP: Install your floor before adding the skirting board, as this makes it possible to conceal any gaps or roughly cut edges.

TIP: When cutting wooden flooring allow an extra piece to fill the doorways. If you cut the floor to fit the room and ignore the doorway you will be left with a space that will need filling to avoid a gap between that and the floor in the next room. If you leave a little extra, you can always trim it back later.

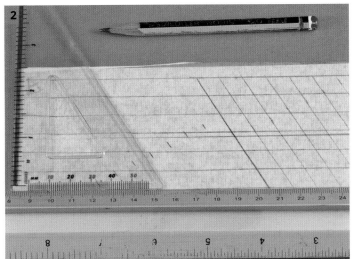

BELOW STAIRS

LEFT Preparations are well underway for a royal banquet in this scene which recreates the kitchens of Brighton's Royal Pavilion.
Maker: Puppenhausmuseum

BELOW LEFT The butler's pantry is where the glass and silverware are kept. Some is out on the table for cleaning, but other precious items are kept under lock and key.
Maker: Emma Waddell

BELOW The secret to every well-functioning house is an adequately stocked larder.
Maker: Ann Taylor

BELOW The maid ensures that everything is tidy in her room before starting the day's work.
Maker: Jacky Miles

ABOVE The butler's bedroom is sparsely decorated, but comfortable.
Maker: Emma Waddell

RIGHT Every day is wash day in the busy laundry of Hill House. Dozens of irons have been left to heat up on the huge iron stove. A series of wooden formers hang on the right-hand wall; they are used to ensure stockings and breeches do not get misshapen while wet.
Maker: Ann Taylor

A 35-year project

With remote-controlled lighting, sound, and smoking chimneys, this miniature version of Rainham Hall shows that even when modelling period properties you can include some very modern elements.

RAINHAM HALL WAS BUILT IN THE 18TH century by merchant John Harle to showcase the various building materials that he imported from Europe. Its miniature cousin might accurately be described as maintaining this tradition, with real marble, lead and brick all being used in places throughout the house. But it is the intricacy of the construction that makes this a truly remarkable house and why it took 35 years to complete.

Built by Geoffrey Walkley for his daughter, it is constructed from half-inch mahogany joined together by lines of mortises and tenons. A set of three-by-three interlocking boxes created the first and second floors and the partition walls between rooms. This meant that the boxes could be slid in and out during construction to make tasks like wiring a little easier. It also results in an incredibly rigid structure. As Geoffrey remarked: 'My son-in-law, Mark, used to joke that the safest place to be in an earthquake would be under the house!'

Snaking its way down through the house from the attic to the front door is a magnificent staircase with curved handrails finishing in a spiral at the foot – all handcrafted in mahogany. Dolls' house staircases are rarely continuous, so the fact that it serves all floors is

ABOVE The facade and porch are exact replicas of Rainham Hall.

'It is the intricacy of the construction that makes this a truly remarkable house.'

RIGHT The salon is the perfect place to receive guests.

noteworthy enough. But siting the staircase was a particular challenge, as it had to avoid running across any of the 45 opening sash windows. It is no wonder that this aspect alone took over a year to build.

Another immensely time-consuming job was the exterior brickwork. There are around 7,000 bricks in total, each hand-carved into the walls of the house and then hand-painted – twice!

Running round the top of the real Rainham Hall is a stone cornice, which Geoffrey was keen to replicate in detail, down to cutting individual dentils. 'It is one of the features, of which I am most proud. The other is the drainpipe hoppers,' he said. These were cast in resin from a wooden master that Geoffrey made (see page 50). Departing slightly from the originals, which are marked with the date of completion, the miniature versions are monogrammed with his daughter's initials. Adding a date was best avoided, as it is not always easy to determine when a project of this scale will be completed.

Inside the detail continues. The library is lined by bookshelves (home to close to 400 books) and features an elaborate parquet floor. There is another patterned wooden floor to be found in the dining room, while one bathroom boasts a design in black and white ceramic tiles.

When it came to installing the electrics, Geoffrey's son-in-law was drafted in for advice. A backbone of multi-core cable runs up through the house, feeding lights, sockets and fires. Each can be turned on and off individually by remote control. A drawer in the base of the house holds an iPod Nano, which feeds a concealed speaker in the music room. A second speaker by the front door connects to a teddy bear growler unit, on which Mark recorded the sound of a Victorian doorbell. Crowning the whole house are 14 chimneys, six of which actually emit smoke.

TOP The library is home to around 400 books.

ABOVE The kitchen features a full battery of copper pots and pans.

LEFT With a marble floor and intricate mahogany staircase, the hall is just one example of how materials have been used to make this a genuinely special house.

Wooden mouldings

Coving, skirting, architrave and dado rails are important finishing touches in a room. They can also hide a multitude of sins, such as the slightly rough edges of a piece of wallpaper. People tend to get a little confused when working out the angle to cut mouldings to go round bends, but careful measuring and using card to make a dummy version helps to get the perfect result every time.

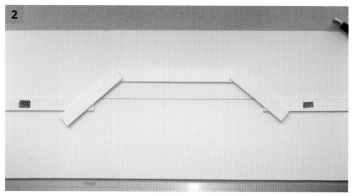

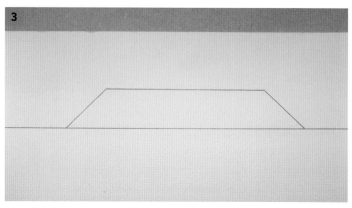

1 Cut strips of card to go around the bay and glue them together. Ensure the strips are tight to the wall and go right into the corners of the bay. This will form your pattern so must be done accurately.

2 Draw a straight line on a piece of card large enough to lay out the whole pattern. This is the line of the wall if it continued straight rather than going into the bay. Hold or pin the pattern on to the card, lining the template up against the straight line of the wall.

3 Carefully draw around the pattern. When you take the pattern away, you should be left with an outline of the bay.

4 Draw the footprint of your chosen moulding on to the card by making parallel lines the width of the moulding inside the outline. Check that the lines are the correct width apart by placing the moulding on to the card, making sure to place the side that would be closest to the ceiling on to the card outline if you are cutting coving; put the side that would be nearest the floor down for skirting.

5 Draw a line through the corners of the template. This gives you the angles that you need to cut. In the picture these lines are shown in red. Place your moulding on to the card the correct way up.

6 Align the end of the moulding just over the red line using the stock of a square against the moulding to ensure it is straight. Mark a line on top of the moulding. Without moving the square, mark the back where the red line meets the moulding and using the square, draw a line from this point to the top. Draw a line across the top of the mark at the front to the one at the back. These are the marks you need to cut to.

7 Hold the moulding with a bench hook and carefully cut along the lines using a razor saw. If you are cutting mouldings for the corner of the room or to go round a chimney breast, you can use a miniature mitre block, which holds the moulding in place and has slits cut out that guide the saw for the most common mitre angles. Take your time when cutting; the harder or faster you push, the more likely the moulding is to jump off line. Once cut, clean any saw marks using a sanding stick, but make sure you do not alter the angle.

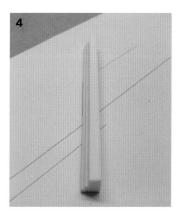

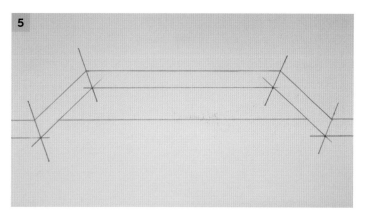

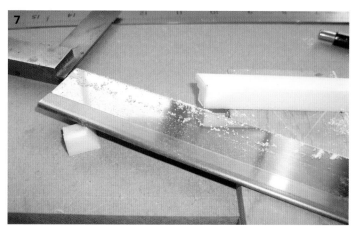

8 Mark and cut all the other sections as described. Glue them together using superglue for resin mouldings, wood glue (wooden mouldings) or PVA glue (plaster). Use the outline on the card as a guide. Adjust the fit by sanding if the pieces do not quite follow the template line.

9 Once all the pieces have been cut, check that they fit your dolls' house by laying the completed moulding on the template.

10 Apply pieces of masking tape either side of the join. This is to protect the moulding and save too much filler sticking to the moulding. In the picture, parcel tape has been used for clarity.

11 Carefully fill the joint with decorator's filler, making sure to push it into the gap. Clean the majority of excess filler following the shape of the moulding.

12 Once the filler has hardened completely, remove the tape. This should leave a minimal amount of filler to sand. Rub the piece down carefully to avoid damaging the shape of the moulding. Paint the moulding and then glue it into place in the house. Use a prop to hold it in place while the glue dries.

TIP: Some modellers like to paint the moulding before marking and cutting. It can be easier to get a smooth finish when painting a long length. The joins will need touching up after cutting.

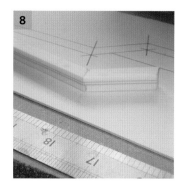

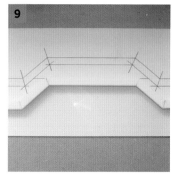

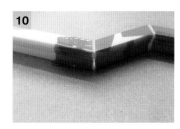

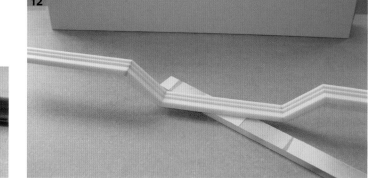

Grand parlour on a small scale

Shiny finishes or strong colours can look overbearing in a small space,
but that intensity is perfect for anyone modelling in the rococo style,
as Annemarie Kwikkel demonstrates.

LOOKING AT THESE PICTURES THERE IS nothing to suggest this rococo parlour is anything other than a salon in Vienna's Hofburg palace. Everything is so exactly proportioned. However, the scene is, in fact, a 1:12 scale room box, inspired by a visit to Vienna and the opulent palaces of the Empress Elisabeth. Miniaturist Annemarie Kwikkel chose the Viennese style because it gave her lots of scope for modelling. 'Rococo-style interiors are so elegant and 'over the top', which is perfect for a miniature version,' she said. Sometimes working in small scale, gold and intense colours can seem overbearing, but the rococo style was all about bling, so it works perfectly.

'It was inspired by a visit to Vienna and the opulent palaces of the Empress Elisabeth.'

ABOVE With gilding and scroll work, this room has been given a truly rococo feel.

She prefers to make room boxes, because they offer greater flexibility than working on an entire house. Each box can be built to a different size, depending on the scene to be recreated. There is also the opportunity to experiment with different ages and styles of room. In a house, you are more or less confined to making a suite of rooms of the same period.

The room box was built from scratch, working from detailed sketches. To create a feeling of space and to ensure there was room for a chandelier to hang from the decorative ceiling, Annemarie wanted to make the box quite tall. This dictated the size and shape of the other main feature of the room – the two bay windows. Once the dimensions for these two elements were set, Annemarie – with the help of her husband – could begin to construct the box, though the ceiling was left off until the last stage to allow space to work and for the ceiling decoration to be completed separately.

The order of construction and decoration is important in any miniature scene. Annemarie tackled the walls first and then moved on to creating the parquetry floor and lastly the ceiling. She had to scour the internet to find the wallpaper, the door, the columns and the lights. 'That took a lot of time because it had to suit the room and I had to make sure it all fitted well together,' she said.

The windows proved a particular challenge. Not only did they have to be of a specific style, they had to be made with great precision to fit the bays. 'That was really fiddly because I was working in millimetres; it all fits exactly,' she said. The chairs pushed back into the bay were a cheap find, but by being re-covered in the same fabric as the curtains and then gilded, they appear the height of luxury.

Casting

Casting an item from a mould allows you to consistently recreate intricate decorative features multiple times. This can be particularly useful when trying to make decorative ceilings, stone swags and pediments where the same details are repeated at multiple points.

CREATING A MOULD

The first step is to create an accurate drawing of the design. This helps you to work out what you are trying to achieve. If drawn to scale, it may also be used as the base upon which to build your master; if you are creating the master from individual elements, it is possible to lay each one down on top of the design to ensure they are the right shape and size.

The master can be made of any medium. Some people carve the master out of wood, or create it in polymer clay; others build the master from a collection of bits and pieces such as wire, beads and jewellery findings.

LEFT A master and the moulded copy.
Maker: Geoffrey Walkley

BELOW It is a good idea to lay the pieces out on your drawing as you create the master.
Maker: Sue Cook

The master is then used to create a mould. These are typically made of latex or silicone, though latex is beginning to fall out of favour because it is harder to work with and some people are allergic to it.

There are two types of silicone moulding material – pourable and putty. Using the former, you will have to build a framework around the master that contains the silicone while it sets. Putty has a clay-like consistency and can simply be pressed around the master and then left to harden. This requires less skill and time than using the pourable variety and, thus, putty is often the better choice for beginners.

The important thing is to press the putty firmly into the master, so that it fits around each of the intricate details. It is best to press the putty into the deepest areas first and to work from the centre outwards to avoid pulling the putty away from the original as you create the mould. The putty should be around ¼in (6mm) deep on all sides of the master to create a solid mould.

MOULDING MATERIALS

The putty is mixed from two base ingredients. Once mixed, you will need to work quickly. Depending on the brand of putty, it can harden in as little as five minutes. As a result, you should only mix the amount that you need for the current project. Do not worry if you run out of putty while covering the master, or if the mould is too thin. Once the first layer is dry, you can add a second coat. Any unused putty must be stored in an airtight container.

The mould can be used to make replicas of items in a range of materials, including plaster and resin. Silicone is resistant to very high temperatures, meaning that it can also be filled with polymer clay that needs to be baked in the oven.

Plaster tends to be brittle and can easily break when being removed from the mould. However, it is the ideal medium for many items like ceiling roses, pilasters and mantelpieces that would often be made of plaster in a full-scale house. Resin works well for most other items as it can easily be painted and made to look like plaster, metal or wood. It can also be

RIGHT Pre-made resin moulding strip can be bent to the shape you need by gently heating it with a hot air gun. It is important to make a template of the shape that you want first, so that you have a guide around which to bend the moulding. The heat should be applied evenly, taking care not to heat any one area for too long or to twist the moulding while bending it.

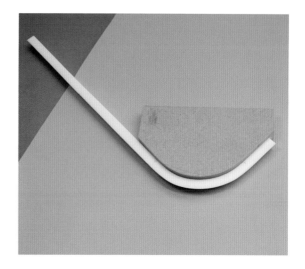

mixed with other materials, such as a small amount of terracotta dust, to achieve textured finishes, for example when making roof tiles.

Resin is mixed from two base ingredients – resin and hardener. You will need to read the pack instructions carefully and measure the quantities of each ingredient accurately. If the mixture is not right, the resin will not set or harden properly. Adding more hardener will not make the mixture set any faster; it may actually stop it hardening fully. Mix thoroughly especially around the sides; you can tell when it is fully mixed because the fluid goes clear with no streaking.

When the plaster or resin has set, you have to be careful releasing it from the mould. It is easy to break delicate items as you are getting them out of the moulds. Even if the items come out of the mould cleanly, you are likely to have some residue between two parts of a casting, e.g. between the arm and the body on a statue, or a seam where two halves of a mould join. These have to be filed down to get a smooth finish.

Once smooth, dipping an item made from resin in acetone will ensure it comes up shiny and white, providing a good surface for painting, though the item will need to be coated with an acrylic primer first.

CASTLES

ABOVE In December 1944, the town of Clervaux, Luxembourg was at the centre of the Battle of the Bulge. US troops stationed at the town's 800-year-old château came under German attack. Claude Joachim trawled post-war archives to be able to recreate the damage wrought by the battle in his 1:35 scale diorama of the town and castle.
Maker: Claude Joachim

BELOW With its beamed ceiling, linen fold panelling and an imposing fireplace, this early 16th-century hall looks every inch the miniature castle. A particularly clever touch is how the dresser to the right has been made to mirror the built-in seat to the left. The high-backed chairs, candelabras, heavy oak table and tapestries enhance the look.
Maker: The Thorne Rooms

ABOVE AND RIGHT Taking inspiration from fantasy, folklore and tales from Anton Pieck, Walt Disney and JK Rowling, Rik Pierce has created a range of miniature towers and castles. Here is his interpretation of Hogwarts School of Witchcraft and Wizardry complete with magical ceiling in the main hall.
Maker: Rik Pierce

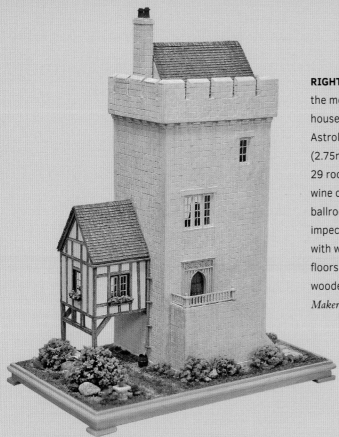

RIGHT Estimated to be the most expensive dolls' house in the world, Astrolat Castle is 9ft (2.75m) tall and houses 29 rooms, including a wine cellar, chapel and a ballroom. Each one is impeccably furnished with wooden parquet floors and hand-etched wooden panels.
Maker: Elaine Diehl

ABOVE The 15th-century Tower House would stand as an imposing entrance to any miniature city. Certainly nothing about it suggests its diminutive stature – built in 1:144 scale. The tower even houses four tiny floors with a single room on each; a fifth room is in the unfortified wooden lodge.
Maker: Nell Corkin

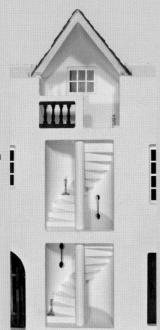

RIGHT Situated in the disputed lands of the Scottish Border Country, this fortified house features many traditional features, including a forestair in a turret. When permission was given to build a house, the canny Scots would build the staircase into a tower at the front to maximize space in all the rooms and sneak a little bit of extra land!
Maker: Jean Nisbett

Wood panelling

From the Tudor period onwards, wood panelling has been a feature of interior decoration in domestic houses particularly in hallways and on stairs. Styles ranged from basic tongue and groove wainscoting to moulded panels and elaborate *boiserie*. Panelled doors were also the norm for many styles of house. You may find it useful to study books on different styles of architecture to find which design was in vogue during your chosen period.

Wood panels are created by gluing bars and panels to a base board.

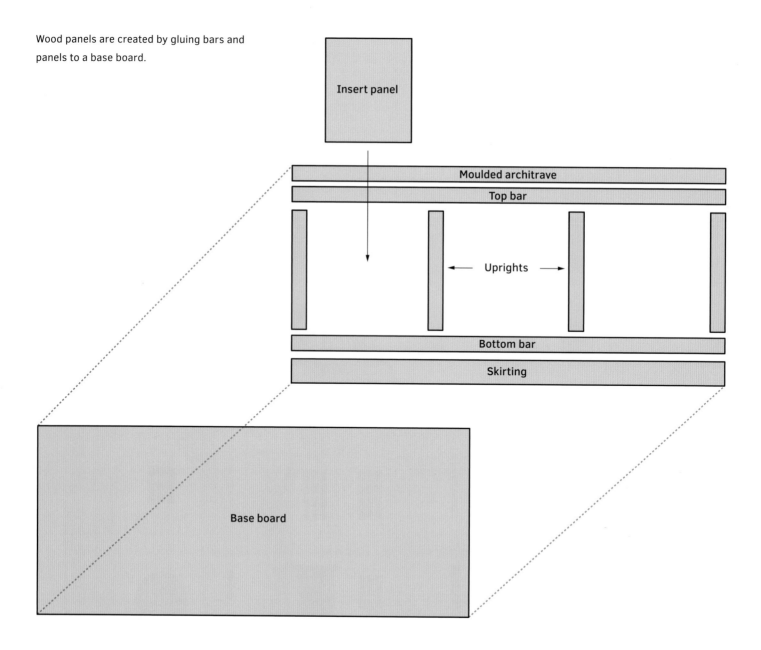

MOULDED PANELS

1 Start by making a base board from plywood about ⅛in (3mm) thick. This should be the size of the area to be panelled.

2 Stain or paint if required. This ensures that you achieve an even coverage across the piece of wood and are not trying to force the paint or dye into corners, risking leaving an uneven finish.

3 Measure and cut a ¹⁄₁₆in (1.5mm) wide strip of wood long enough to run along the full width of the panel. This will make the top part of the moulding frame. For the bottom bar of the frame you will need a strip of the same length that is cut from a strip of wood ¹⁄₁₆in (1.5mm) wider than your chosen skirting. It is a good idea to stain or paint the strip wood as a single bar before cutting.

4 Measure and cut several ¹⁄₁₆in (1.5mm) wide strips of wood to form the uprights. These should be the same length as the distance between the upper and lower bar.

5 Glue the strips on to the base board. Start with the top and bottom edges and fit the uprights in between.

6 For the panelling, use rectangles of ¹⁄₁₆in (1.5mm) plywood to fit the areas between the beading strips, leaving an even-sized gap all around to simulate a router groove – about ¹³⁄₆₄in (5mm) works well.

7 Measure and cut a piece of moulded architrave the length of the base board to run on top of the panelling and give it a neat finish.

8 Glue the panel to the wall.

9 Measure and cut a piece of skirting board. Paint or stain it to match the panelling. Once dry, glue it into place over the bottom bar of the panel.

TIP: Make wainscoting by cutting a series of identical length strips and gluing them side-by-side on a base board, to cover the width of the area to be panelled. Finish with a length of moulded architrave along the top, as before.

TIP: For panelled doors, make the basic plywood door (see Windows and doors, pages 28–29) and then follow the instructions above.

RIGHT Panelling looks particularly good running up the side of the stairs.
Maker: Geoffrey Walkley

DOMESTIC BLISS

EVERY NOW AND AGAIN YOU COME across a miniature home that is very similar to the life-sized one that you have owned at some point in your life and this can be the starting point for a project.

For Jan Simpson Gilman, that item was a mangle similar to the one that her mother owned in the 1940s. It inspired her to recreate the mid-terraced house where she lived as a child, complete with all its conveniences and inconveniences.

The cooker was tucked in a corner behind the door from the hall, while the draining board extended across the back door when in use, making it impossible to go out into the garden. She did employ a little licence – the dressing table in her miniature bedroom is closer to the one that she would have wanted, rather than the one she was actually allowed by her parents to have.

For Christine Bloxham, the starting point was a household inventory listing the possessions of merchant Edward Wood that she discovered while researching her family history.

Taking inspiration from a real-life property or event has the advantage that you know exactly the look and feel that you are trying to create with your project. However, having found one or two items that

OPPOSITE Interested in decorating, antiques and history, Christine-Léa Frisoni had a habit of changing the decor in her house very regularly until she found an outlet to do it in miniature.
Maker: Christine-Léa Frisoni

look exactly like the ones you used to own, you may then have a challenge on your hands to source other items that closely resemble your full-sized possessions.

Whatever the era chosen, the dolls' houses featured in this chapter reveal a growing tendency to move away from the grand houses that modellers would love to own, but could never really afford, to something on a more domestic scale. They represent the style of house in which many people of the day would have lived, not the castles and palaces of the few.

Practicality plays a large part. Very few people have the space to accommodate a miniature mansion within their own home. They are also expensive and time consuming to build.

Once you have the miniature bug, it is very common to go from one project to another, trying first one scale, period or style of property before moving on to another – not least because it is easy to be attracted at a miniatures fair to items on sale that cannot possibly be incorporated within the current project because they are the wrong style or from the wrong era.

Scaling things down means you may have a much greater chance of completing a dolls' house within a few years and can then move on to indulge your desire to create something quite different.

PERIOD HOMES

BELOW While researching her family history, Christine Bloxham came across an inventory for the house of her ancestor Edward Wood, a merchant from Macclesfield, UK. The list was the starting point for creating her merchant's house. Visits to historic houses furnished in the 17th-century style helped to shape ideas for the parlour.
Maker: Christine Bloxham

ABOVE While predominantly Georgian, this house shows there is no need to 'stick to the rules'. All the pieces of furniture in the house are replicas of real furniture. The harpsichord made by Tony Scammell is a replica of one that Mozart used.
Maker: Karon Lesley

LEFT Having bought a Sid Cooke dolls' house kit, Deborah Newell's ambition was to create an authentic Georgian house. This elegant lounge certainly seems to fit the bill.
Maker: Deborah Newell

LEFT A fan of Jane Austen, Roz Clackett decided to recreate Longbourn, the Bennett family house as it appeared in the BBC television series *Pride and Prejudice*. The room is simply furnished reflecting their status as a family 'of the middling sort'.
Maker: Roz Clackett

RIGHT A gentleman's study is the ideal place to display curiosities that take the collector's fancy, but might find no other place in the dolls' house. Medals, coins, butterflies and fossils are just some of the paraphernalia that can be displayed.
Maker: Carol Black

Painting and decorating

When it comes to decorating a miniature house, you face many of the same choices as you do with full-scale interior decoration. Firstly, you need to think about what colour each room will be and then whether to paint, tile or wallpaper it. Once you have decided on the colour scheme, complete as much of the painting before assembly as you can, as it is not easy to work in cramped spaces.

HANGING WALLPAPER

1 Accurately measure the vertical height of the room and cut the paper to size. Make sure the paper is straight and the pattern runs vertically. Do not worry if this means the top and bottom edges are not quite straight as these will be covered by the skirting board and cornice. Pay attention to the pattern repeat, as you will want the design to match up across drops. With large patterns, this may mean wasting half the sheet because the pattern does not repeat very often. Sheets of wallpaper vary in size, but generally you will need one sheet of paper for each wall, or two half sheets if you are having different designs top and bottom separated by a dado rail. Leave extra on the width and trim it later. Label the wallpaper piece for each wall and add an arrow to indicate the top of the paper. Work from key features such as chimney breasts outwards.

At the corner of the room, you can cut the paper and start with another piece of paper on the next wall but this can leave a small gap unless you cut accurately. Alternatively, you can turn 13⁄64in (5mm) of the wallpaper round the corner on to the next wall and apply the new piece of paper over the top, but this may leave a slight bump. This is less visible if you paper the back wall first and apply the paper for the side wall over the top.

2 Apply the paste or glue. By pasting the paper and leaving it to soak for a few minutes it becomes supple and easy to hang. By pasting the wall, the paper will slide easily into position. It is worth experimenting with the approach that works best for you. When applying paste to the paper brush out from the centre, ensuring that all the edges are pasted.

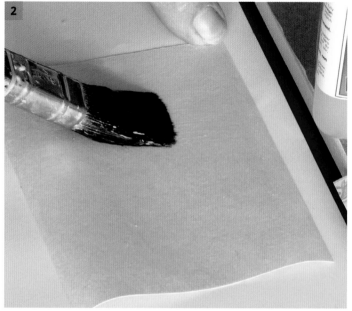

PAINTING

Commercially produced dolls' house kits are normally made of wood or MDF. When painting the walls it is important to choose the right paint for the base medium and to treat it as you would if painting woodwork or furniture in your own home. It is not always necessary to prime the walls, but MDF is particularly absorbent and will take a lot of paint on the first coat. Priming with a coat of Gesso or specialist MDF primer will give you a good base to work on.

A lot of dolls' house makers use emulsion for interior walls. It is readily available as tester pots in a range of colours; some brands produce specialist heritage paints that are good if you are modelling a period property. Pick a paint that has an eggshell or vinyl silk finish. Matt paints tend to look too flat and chalky; a gloss finish tends to look too shiny in a small space. Gloss is fine to use on skirting boards and doors; it is just not right for walls. Alternatively, acrylic is a good option for skirting and furniture, but needs finishing with a layer of clear varnish to give it the appropriate sheen.

When decorating, it is best to apply paint lightly. Two or three thin coats will always give a better finish than one thick one. It also makes it easier to avoid getting paint in any of the joints and grooves, which can cause problems with slotting the pieces of the kit together tightly. It also increases the chance of the paint leaking into a neighbouring room and spoiling earlier hard work.

3 Hang the wallpaper. You will need a soft cloth or clean brush to gently rub out any air bubbles. Get the paper as flat as possible and keep gently pushing any turned-up corners down until they stick – again work from the middle outwards. A wallpaper seam roller is useful to press down the edges; only press very lightly and do not roll textured or embossed wallpaper. Do not worry if there is a bit of stretching as most of it will come out as the paper dries.

The thicker the paper, though, the less it will stretch. Wait for the paste to dry completely (at least 24 hours) before trimming any excess paper with a sharp knife. Wet paper is difficult to cut with a knife and prone to tearing, but it can be trimmed with scissors if necessary.

TIP: Paint the ceiling before you wallpaper. It is more difficult to do once the wallpaper is hung, because of the risk of splashes. Consider turning the house upside down, so that you are working with gravity rather than above your head.

TIP: Wire and test the lights before wallpapering, but then remove them. If they remain *in situ* while you are decorating, you will constantly knock them and cause damage.

TIP: Hang any wallpaper before adding the skirting board, door architraves and cornice, as this makes it possible to conceal any gaps or roughly cut edges.

20TH-CENTURY HOMES

RIGHT Katina Beale believes her house 'chose her'. She knew she did not want a Victorian or Edwardian property, but was immediately taken by a 1:24 Art Deco home with roof terrace.

Maker: Katina Beale

BELOW Katina Beale fitted an American-style 1930s kitchen, which at the time would have been the height of modernity and sophistication.

Maker: Katina Beale

RIGHT Having identified the style of furniture she wanted in books and magazines and from television programmes, Katina Beale spent days trawling the internet looking for the right thing. The sideboard was inspired by one used in the UK television series *Poirot*.

Maker: Katina Beale

ABOVE To replicate the family's belongings exactly, most of the furniture had to be made from scratch or adapted from kits. The three-piece suite is covered with dolls' house self-adhesive carpet fabric to give the impression of uncut moquette. The edges were then 'piped' with bunka.
Maker: Jan Simpson Gilham

ABOVE Working from old family photo albums, Jan Simpson Gilham recreated the 1930s mid-terraced house that she lived in until the age of 22. There is a blank side wall where the adjoining house would have been.
Maker: Jan Simpson Gilham

RIGHT A view of the interior with the back wall removed. Items were placed exactly where they would have been in Jan Simpson Gilham's childhood home, so unusually we see the back of the lavatory cistern and basin.
Maker: Jan Simpson Gilham

Playing to the gallery

This arts-and-crafts inspired library shows that by modifying
a shop-bought kit, you can achieve stunning and unique results.

MINIATURISTS ARE ADEPT AT 'KIT
bashing' – taking a kit and adapting it to fit the
design of their house and to make it more in keeping
with a particular period. But in a move that is not
for the faint-hearted, Josje Veenenbos cut a hole in
the ceiling of one room. She wanted to connect the
study to the room above, where she planned to build
a library, like the galleried libraries she had seen in
some period properties.

That is where the fun started... There is a cosy
corner next to the fireplace in the study where a
person could sit and read but, before they could settle
down, they had to be able to fetch a book, which
meant getting upstairs to the library floor. This
necessitated a staircase going up through the opening,
but one that would not take up much floor space in
either room (in the gallery there is only enough floor
space at the edge to access each of the bookshelves)
or crowd the hole where she wanted to hang a
chandelier on a long chain.

The answer was a spiral staircase built around a
central brass rod. It took a lot of measuring to work
out the height of the steps, the direction of the spiral
and the location of the stairs to maximize space in
both rooms. Josje even 'employed' a doll to walk up
and down the stairs to make sure it was possible to
go up and down without bumping your head!

In the upper room, a galleried area has been
created by adding a balustrade made from curtain
poles and some fencing materials found in a model
railway shop. The walls are lined with handmade
bookshelves and over 1,000 books. The shelves under
the windows are hidden behind curtains – disguising
the fact that the shelves are empty until more books
can be made.

RIGHT A hole has been cut in the ceiling to create
a galleried library above.

'Josje even "employed" a doll to walk up and down the stairs to make sure it was possible.'

ABOVE LEFT AND RIGHT Downstairs there are cosy corners where the owner can work or read a book.

LEFT Upstairs, the walls are lined with thousands of books. There is just enough room to walk around the gallery to choose a volume.

Tiled floors

Tiles are one of the most common types of flooring, particularly in bathrooms, kitchens and hallways. They are particularly prized for being easy to keep clean. In the Victorian era, with the advent of encaustic tiles, much more elaborate patterns began to emerge incorporating shaped tiles and patterned insets. Once you have mastered the basic technique, patterns are easy to achieve – it just needs a little planning and experimentation. As with other types of flooring, tiled floors should be built outside the house and slid into place once completed.

LAYING INDIVIDUAL TILES

1 Make a template to the dimensions of your floor following the instructions for laying wood flooring (see Wood flooring, pages 38-39). Mark the centre line on your floor template and calculate how many of your chosen tiles will fit across it. You want to avoid ending up with small slivers of tile on one side of the room; if using slate, terracotta or ceramic tiles, small pieces will be difficult to cut and will be prone to breaking. It is better to have to cut the tiles on both sides of the room, such that there is two-thirds of a tile at each edge rather than having a full tile on one side and a tiny strip on the other.

2 Make sure the surface on which you will be laying the tiles is clean and dry. If using real terracotta or ceramic tiles, remove any loose bits from the underside of the tile with a clean, damp cloth.

3 Begin laying the tiles. Work from your centre line outwards. Apply PVA glue to each tile individually and lay in place. Alternatively apply PVA to a small area of floor and place tiles into position. If you intend to grout your floor then remember to allow a ³⁄₆₄in (1mm) gap between tiles for mortar joints. Allow to dry.

TIP: Before gluing or cutting, experiment with the position of the tiles by moving them around on the template until you achieve the best layout.

TIP: Terracotta and soft stone tiles can be cut with a craft knife. Simply score then snap over a straight edge. Alternatively use pincers or tile pliers. To cut real slate or harder stone, score both sides of the tile with a craft knife and then snap between your fingers, or use tile pliers or a junior hacksaw (in this case a dust mask should be worn for protection). Slate tiles may

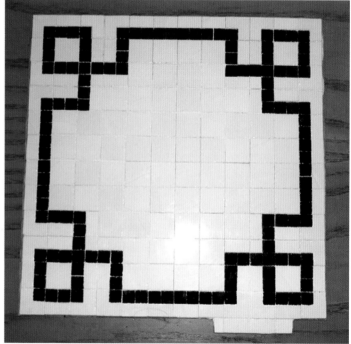

differ slightly in thickness; reserve the thinnest tiles for the edges as these will be easier to cut. Shape tiles by rubbing on a medium-grade abrasive paper. Vinyl tiles can be cut to size using scissors.

TOP AND ABOVE Tiled floors should be created outside the house and then slotted in.
Maker: Geoffrey Walkley

FINISHING THE FLOOR

1 If using slate, or terracotta tiles, once you have tiled the entire floor, wipe the surface of the tiles with a damp cloth to remove any dust. Mix equal parts of PVA and water together and using a brush, paint this over your tiles. Allow to dry before proceeding. Your tiles are now ready for grouting.

2 Mix the grout to a paste; it should be smooth and resemble thick cream. Apply liberally, making sure you get it into all gaps. Use a damp sponge and wipe the excess off on the surface of the tiles. This takes time. Keep rinsing the sponge regularly in a bowl of water, then wring it out until it is almost dry and wipe the surface again. Use a dry cloth to buff off any remaining residue.

3 Slide the floor into place.

ABOVE Tiles are one of the most common types of flooring, particularly in kitchens, bathrooms and hallways.

LEFT A real marlstone floor from Richard Stacey has been laid in this laundry.
Maker: Emma Waddell

BELOW Real terracotta tiles have been used in this kitchen.
Maker: Geoffrey Walkley

FRENCH TOWN HOUSES

ABOVE, RIGHT AND BELOW The addition of curtains on the armoire and the faded flower motifs on the bed and chest, lend a French rustic charm to this room.

Maker: Sue Kendell

RIGHT With its pastel blues, soft pinks and generally muted, dusty tone, this desk could grace any French château.
Maker: Matthew Weston

LEFT Renate Stettler treated each miniature with antique finishes and worked in a pastel colour palette throughout to create a consistent and coherent feel to her French property.
Maker: Renate Stettler

Gay Paree

Linda Carswell has incorporated elements from different buildings she has seen on trips to France to create a house that exudes Gallic charm.

ABOVE AND LEFT Linda Carswell was aiming for a chic sophisticated style in this French-inspired dolls' house.

LINDA CARSWELL WANTED A CHIC DOLLS' house that would elegantly enhance the decor in her own home – not look like something that a child might own. With a love of France, there was no other choice but a Parisian-style townhouse and, armed with a mass of photographs from various trips to France, she set out to build one from scratch.

She started by designing the house on graph paper, so that she could work out how to incorporate the elements from different French properties she had photographed. 'I found and photographed pretty balconies in Paris and Chinon, roof style and shape

ABOVE Louis XV-style furniture gives this corner a truly French feel.

from other buildings, chimneys from another,' she said. The drawings were then scaled up to work out the exact dimensions of the 1:12 scale miniature mansion. Her husband David helped with the construction of the shell of the house, but after that Linda completed the construction and decoration herself.

For the interior, she wanted a look that was soft and elegant, but also timeless. 'I didn't want it to look as though it was from any particular era,' she explained. Again she worked from photos, taking individual design ideas from each. Inspired by the muted blue and white tiles she saw in one house, she decided to make some from wood. They are all individually painted, sanded and then glued on to graph paper before being fitted into the hall. Likewise, the parquet floor is a copy of a design from a French interiors magazine.

Most of the furniture is built from kits, so that she could adapt it to style of the house. Many of the pieces have been painted a soft white to create a subtle aged effect. 'I find that it is important when working in miniature that you do not allow any one item to overpower or take over a room; it is all about balance and harmony.'

This desire for harmony means that Linda has many spare pieces of furniture that have been removed from the house. She photographs each room regularly throughout the decoration to see if everything looks balanced and works together. If an item stands out, then it is taken away. Truly, the camera never lies!

TOP AND ABOVE The floor tiles were made from individual squares of painted wood.

'For the interior, she wanted a look that was soft and elegant, but also timeless.'

Curtains

Make a set of full-length Georgian-style curtains for your dolls' house.

1 Using the template, cut the pelmet facing panel from a piece of thick card. It should be wide enough to cover the width of your window and frame. Cut a rectangle of card for the top of the pelmet that is 1in (25mm) wide and the same length as your pelmet facing panel.

2 Cut two squares of cardboard 1 x 1in (25 x 25mm) and make a 25/64in (10mm) hole in the middle of each. Cover each piece in fabric. You will need about a 25/64in (10mm) overhang so that you can fold and glue the fabric to the wrong side. Cut notches and slits to help the fabric fit around the corners and curves.

3 Once the glue has dried, glue the top rectangle to the pelmet facing panel along the long edge, making sure the right sides of the fabric are on the outside. Once this is dry, attach the side squares.

4 Make a template for the curtains that is the width of your top frame and 25/64in (10mm) longer than the distance between the curtain mounting and the floor. Use the template to cut two rectangles of lining fabric and two of your chosen curtain fabric. Use

pinking shears to cut them out as this will reduce fraying. Make a 13/64in (5mm) hem around all four sides of each piece by first pressing it and then sewing it. Place the lining on top of the curtain fabric with the wrong sides together. Sew along the top of the curtains about 9/32in (7mm) down from the top. Repeat for the second curtain. You should now have two lined curtains. Mark 19/32in (15mm) intervals along the top of the curtains on the back for the rings.

5 Attach rings to the curtains by making tiny holes with an awl where you marked the intervals. Open up your rings with pliers and thread them through the holes. Close the links. Fold pleats into your curtains and set them with an iron. Thread your curtains on to a pole and insert them into the pelmet that you made earlier. They should rest nicely through the 25/64in (10mm) holes in the side.

6 To make the curtain ties, fold the fabric in half and use the template to cut four pieces. Place two pieces with the right sides together and stitch around the outside, leaving a 13/64in (5mm) seam allowance. Leave one of the short ends

open. Turn them the right way out; you may need pliers for this. Stitch the short ends together to create a loop and snip the seam with pinking shears to stop fraying. Turn the ties so the seam is on the inside. Add to your curtains.

TIP: Embellish your pelmet by sticking a series of card triangles layered on top of each other to create an art deco style. Or make a lace edge for a country cottage.

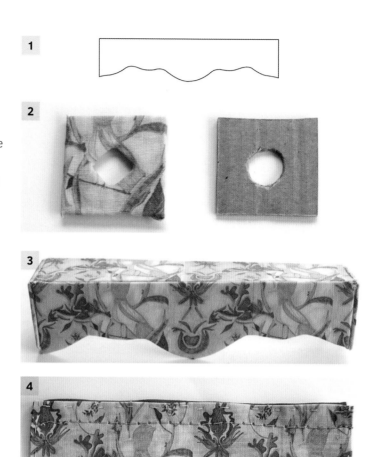

Bedding

Get ready for bed with a set of simple sheets and pillows.

MATTRESS

1 Cut a foam pad to fit the size of the bed from 2in (50mm) thick foam. If you are working on a bed that has a solid head and/or foot, you will want to make the mattress slightly smaller than the base of the bed, as the sheets and blankets will take up some thickness at the head and the foot.

2 Cover the foam pad with white or striped cotton.

SHEETS

1 Cut a rectangle of fine cotton batiste. It should be big enough to tuck under the mattress all the way around. This will form the bottom sheet.

2 Hem the fabric. It is good to form it with an iron, then sew it in place or apply a fine line of glue with the tip of a cocktail stick and press it shut.

3 Pleat the corners of the sheet neatly over the mattress and hold in place with glue or hidden stitches.

4 Cut a second rectangle of cotton batiste. It should be about 2in (50mm) shorter than the first piece, but should still be wide enough to tuck under the mattress. This will form the top sheet. Hem as before, adding lace or a thin line of ribbon to the top edge, if desired.

5 Place it over the base sheet and pleat the corners as before.

TIP: Blankets are made in the same way as the top sheet.

PILLOWS

1 Fold a piece of ticking in half. Measure and cut two pieces of ticking 1⅜ x 2¹¹⁄₆₄in (35 x 55mm). The stripes should run parallel with the short edge.

2 Sew the bottom and sides leaving a ⅛in (3mm) seam allowance. Be sure to leave a gap to insert the stuffing.

3 Trim the corners diagonally outside the stitching lines to remove excess fabric then turn the pillows the right way out.

4 Stuff the pillow with fibrefill and hand sew the gap closed. Small white beads also work well as they are heavy and can be moulded to give a realistic shape to the pillow.

5 Fold a piece of fine cotton batiste in half. Cut two pillowcases. These need to be about ²⁵⁄₆₄in (10mm) larger than your pillow, i.e. 1⁴⁹⁄₆₄ x 2⁹⁄₁₆in (45 x 65mm).

6 Open out your rectangle and sew or glue along one of the longer plain cut edges to make a hem. You can also add a lace trim along this edge.

7 Fold the fabric over with the wrong sides together. Sew the remaining two cut edges together, but not the hemmed side.

8 Turn the pillow right sides out, and check the fit with the pillow. If it is too big, you can re-hem one side to make it smaller.

TIP: Use a good-quality fabric and iron well so that no creases remain. Cotton is much more forgiving than silk and easier to work with. Hems can be glued rather than sewn, but never glue any part of the fabric where the glue will be visible. However, silk has a wonderful lustre and hangs better once you learn how to work with it.

Upholstery

Ensure your armchairs match your decor by making them and covering them yourself. Alternatively, you could re-upholster an existing chair.

1 Cut a rebate around the top edge of the seat back to make space for padding. It does not need to be very tidy; it just needs to be straight.

2 Measure the base and cut a piece of fabric to go all the way around the bottom. It will need to be ³⁄₆₄in (10mm) wider than the finished depth to allow for it to be glued on to the base of the chair and to accommodate a ¹⁵⁄₆₄in (6mm) hem. It should also be 3⁵⁄₃₂in (80mm) longer than the circumference of the chair to leave enough fabric for the corner pleats. Hem and then glue the fabric to the base, starting in the centre and being careful to align any pattern with the centre of the chair. Create the box pleats in each corners. To keep these in place, make a small stitch at the top of each pleat then place dots of glue inside the pleats, being careful to put glue only on the doubled fabric so that the glue does not leak through.

3 Make a template of the front of the arms and cut out a piece of fabric allowing a little extra so that it folds around the top and sides. You can always cut away any excess fabric later.

4 Cut a piece of interlining a little shorter than the depth of the chair that goes from the top of the arm down the inside of the chair. For a really padded chair, you may want to add a second layer particularly down the sides. Cut a piece of fabric wider than the interlining and fold it over at the front. Starting at the front of the arm, glue the fabric to the chair, sandwiching the layers of interlining. Again be careful to match the pattern as closely as possible. Trim any excess fabric away.

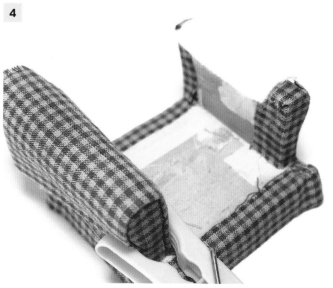

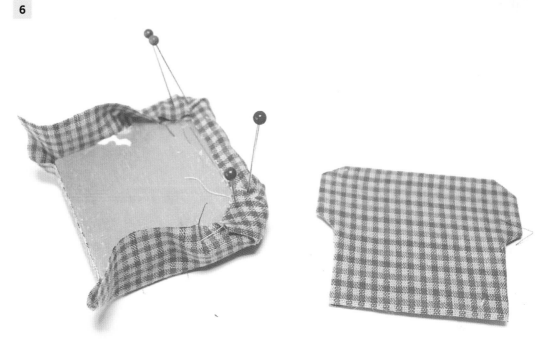

5 Cut and glue a layer of interlining to the inside back. Cut a second layer that also folds over the rebate to make a soft roll at the top of the back and sides. Glue the fabric in place with neat pleats in the corners. Again, cut away any excess fabric.

6 Make a cardboard template for the outside of the chair back. Cover with fabric and then glue over the back to conceal the edges. The seat should be covered in the same way as the back, tucking all edges under and then covering them with a piece of fabric glued to the underside.

7 Finish the sides by covering the unfinished edge with a piece of shaped card covered in fabric and glued firmly under the bulge of the arm.

TIP: Bear in mind that if you are re-covering an existing chair, you may need to deconstruct it. This could mean carefully prising certain elements apart with a chisel. In doing so, cut as much of the old fabric away as possible.

MODERN ROMANCE

TRADITIONALLY, DOLLS' HOUSE enthusiasts have tended to look backwards, recreating beautiful homes from past eras, particularly the Georgian and Victorian periods. Many still do focus on these periods, as there is a wealth of furniture and accessories available, whether mass manufactured, handmade by artisans or in kit form. However, there is a vibrant and growing niche of modellers focusing on contemporary properties.

Embarking on a contemporary modelling project also allows the miniaturist to create a house that feels more familiar. All of us are much more used to houses that contain flat-screen televisions, fridges, microwaves and power showers than ones where the only form of lighting is candles and where the evening's entertainment is a game of cards or a harpsichord recital.

As a result, it may be easier to create rooms that look convincing and realistic. There may be less need for research to find a collection of miniatures that work well together aesthetically.

Joelle Sheard-Patrick talks about having been 'stuck in a bit of a Georgian/Victorian rut'. Buying a mid-century modern house allowed her to explore a whole new period, learning about styles and designers such as Eames and Arne Jacobsen with whom she had previously been unfamiliar.

OPPOSITE With its minimalist decor and deep blue walls, the bedroom in Megan Hornbecker's modernist house exudes urban cool. *Maker: Megan Hornbecker*

As with older styles of house, there is still the opportunity to create a dream home that you could not afford or may simply never be able to inhabit.

The pages of home decoration magazines are fully of sleek, uncluttered rooms that look beautiful, but may be highly impractical. It is hard to maintain clean, unbroken lines, when the children could come home at any point and deposit their school bag or sports kit on the floor. A wealth of toiletries means that bathrooms are rarely without clutter, while kitchen appliances are in use so often that they are left on the side rather than hidden in cupboards.

It may be an exploration into a different style that you like, but would not want to live in. That designer chair or bed may look beautiful, but in reality it would be uncomfortable.

Recreating it in small scale means you can enjoy looking at a piece of furniture, without ever having to suffer the discomfort of actually having to use it.

And do not forget that, just as in real life, the modern miniaturist can have a modern home with funky contemporary furniture set in a period property complete with architectural details such as cornices and fireplaces, or mix vintage finds with the latest styling trends.

MODERNIST AND MINIMALIST HOUSES

LEFT Self-proclaimed 'miniac' Mel Sebastian specializes in creating miniatures that radiate sophistication. Here, she has used a limited colour palette and a few structural pieces to create a stylish contemporary lounge.
Maker: Mel Sebastian, Mad Missy Minis

ABOVE Modelling modern houses gives miniaturists the licence to include furniture from any era, such as this 1960s-inspired credenza. The assumption is that the homeowner is an antiques collector or a fan of vintage furniture.
Maker: Carol Cranmer

LEFT The clean, elegant lines of the mid-century modern furniture and the use of recessed lights create an illusion of space in this room box.
Maker: Peter Tucker

ABOVE Kristine Hanna designed the basin and tap to experiment with 3D printing. The tap was printed in several media, but eventually stainless steel was considered to give the most authentic look and feel for a modern bathroom.
Maker: Kristine Hanna, Paperdollminiatures.com

RIGHT Only a chest of drawers separates the bedroom from the ensuite bathroom with its multi-function rainfall shower.
Maker: Megan Hornbecker

RIGHT Unable to source the modern accessories she craved, Megan Hornbecker turned to 3D printing to create the display of African and Asian art in the TV and entertainment room.
Maker: Megan Hornbecker

Sleek and contemporary solution to scale challenges

A decision to install furniture in a slightly larger scale than the house itself was a gamble that ultimately paid off.

LEFT AND BELOW LEFT Joelle Sheard-Patrick used a consistent palette to give a sleek, contemporary feel.

ABOVE In furnishing the house, Joelle Sheard-Patrick had to work on the principle that less is more and not create too much clutter.

JOELLE SHEARD-PATRICK WAS GIVEN HER first dolls' house at the age of five in 1980 and started building houses from kits in the 1990s, but it was not until 2010 that she discovered the emerging world of modern miniatures. This was largely thanks to the online blogs of fellow miniaturists Christine Ferrara and Megan Hornbecker.

The former also brought the Brinca Dada Emerson House to her attention. And that was it: 'I was smitten after seeing the pictures, and it didn't take me long to place an order for the house,' she said. The design is based on a real house – the Kaufmann Desert House – that was designed by Richard Neutra in the 1940s for retail tycoon Edgar J Kaufmann.

Unusually, the kit was supplied ready painted, so it just needed to be assembled. All the electrics had been installed too, including LED lights powered by a solar panel. However, that did not mean that the house was without challenge.

The 1:16 scale is not particularly common. Joelle spent a long time searching for furniture and talking to makers about the idea of installing 1:12 furniture in a 1:16 house, before taking the leap. 'Doing that was definitely a gamble,' she said. The furniture could easily have looked too big, dominating the space and jarring with the clean lines of the exterior.

The important thing was to stick to using 1:12 throughout and to respect the house's mid-century modern design when choosing pieces. She had to espouse the principle of 'less is more', installing only a select number of sleek and contemporary items. She also had to stick to a consistent palette, occasionally punctuated by bold oranges, reds and greens. The rich mahogany tones of the wooden furniture were specifically chosen to reflect the chocolate colour of the walls.

Furnishing the property became an education in modern art, introducing Joelle to iconic names like Arne Jacobsen and Le Corbusier and to design classics like the Eames and REAC Japan chairs.

ABOVE The house proved an education in mid-century furniture styles.

'Furnishing the property became an education in modern art.'

She also found it inspiring and liberating. Like many dolls' house hobbyists, she felt that she had been stuck in the 'Georgian/Victorian rut'. The ready availability of period houses and furnishings means that many miniaturists do not venture beyond recreating an historic property. 'It's unfortunate. So it was nice to try something outside of my comfort zone,' she commented.

BELOW The house fully opens to reveal the inside.

Remote control

Thanks to modern technology, controlling the lights in your miniature house at the touch of a button may be easier than you anticipate.

OFF-THE-SHELF SOLUTION

If you have a front-opening house and the most convenient socket in your home is behind your dolls' house, using a wireless remote controlled plug is a neat way to save you from reaching around your house every time you want to switch on the lights.

A wireless remote controlled plug is a ready-made unit that is supplied with its own dedicated remote control; a smart plug is the same, but can be operated by your smartphone. The units are designed for use with small household appliances like table lamps, so they are easy to find in electrical stores or online.

Resembling an international power adaptor, the unit plugs straight into a mains wall socket. Once you insert the plug coming from your power supply, it becomes possible to turn the power to your dolls' house on or off using the remote control.

It is a relatively basic solution as all the lights in the house are activated with a single push of a button and you can't turn lights in different rooms on and off separately. However, the units are relatively inexpensive. There is no need to get involved in complex wiring and, therefore, no worry that you have made any costly mistakes. If you buy the right plug for your region, you can be confident that it is suitable for use with your local power supply.

ABOVE A plug-in remote control unit is a simple and inexpensive solution for controlling the lights.

BELOW Programmable remote control units are available if you are feeling more adventurous.

DEDICATED REMOTE CONTROL UNIT

If you are keen to control all your lights independently, then your alternative is to consider a programmable remote control kit, such as that supplied by Micro Miniatures. This includes a remote control handset, a printed circuit board (PCB) and an infrared receiver, which connects to the PCB.

This approach requires that each room in the house has separate wires running to it. The wires from one room, including ceiling and wall lights and the glowing bulbs fitted in a fireplace, may be combined into a single output which goes to the PCB, so that everything in that room is switched on together. Alternatively you could put lights, sockets and fires on separate outputs so that they can be operated independently. When wiring up each room, you must be mindful of how many bulbs are being combined into a single output.

Each channel can safely control up to four bulbs. A typical 24-channel controller could, therefore, operate close to 100 bulbs. In the rare instance that you have more bulbs than this in your house, it is possible to connect a 'slave' unit, which provides an extra 24 channels on top of those in the main unit.

The wires from the lights all need to run to a central point underneath or at the back of your house where the PCB is mounted. This is typically next to the connection to the power supply.

The PCB features a row of individually numbered connections – a total of 24 in the case of a 24-channel controller. The wires from each light or each room are inserted into these connections. The numbered connections correspond to the buttons on the handset, i.e. the light wired to connection 1 will turn on and off when you press button 1 on the handset, and so on.

You will also need to think about where you place the infrared receiver. It is important that it is not covered or obscured in any way; there needs to

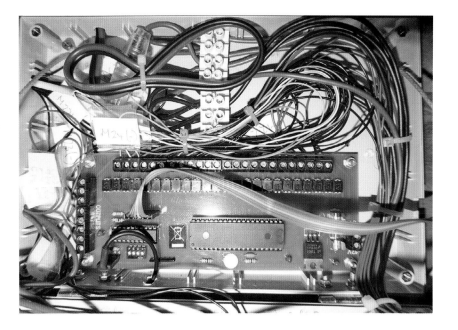

be direct line of sight between the remote control handset and the receiver for the signal to be sent from one to the other. It typically comes with a reasonable length of wire attached, so that it can be connected to the PCB, but fitted in a different and more convenient location.

To complete the circuit, the PCB must be connected to the power supply for the house. This must be rated at 12V DC.

TIPS AND TRICKS

Before connecting the PCB to the lights emanating from the various rooms in your house, it is a good idea to test it with a couple of spare bulbs so that you can get a sense of how the remote controlled unit works.

It also gives you the opportunity to experiment with the programming capability and to work out how to control groups of lights together that are wired to separate connections. In addition to turning each room on and off individually, it is possible to programme default settings. You might want it so that all the lights come on at once when you first switch on the power to the house, or to ensure that items like smoke generators do not come on automatically, but only when you are there to enjoy them.

However, remote control also gives you the opportunity to create particular moods. You might want to group the kitchen, lounge, hall and upstairs landing together. These rooms can be lit up simultaneously, giving the impression that somebody has come home from work and is relaxing downstairs, watching television or making dinner, but has not gone upstairs to bed. As a result, fitting a remote control really can be the gateway to creating a realistic miniature world.

RIGHT The remote control eye needs to be placed somewhere discreet, but visible.

Living in a box

The trend for converting shipping containers into chic modern living spaces has also reached the world of miniatures.

PREFABRICATED CONTAINER HOMES ARE increasingly seen as the answer to many housing problems in the real world, particularly the lack of affordable housing for the young.

When Marion Russek was looking for a contemporary project, she felt a container house was an obvious thing to try and emulate in miniature. But despite their rectangular shape, a shipping container is not as easy to build as it would first appear.

Marion always initiates her projects by designing them in Live Interior Software 3D first. Principally, this allows her to see whether they will be practical to furnish. For example, she can set the size and location of windows so that there is sufficient space along one

LEFT AND BELOW Using 3D interior design software, Marion Russek carefully planned the interior, ensuring there was space for kitchen, bedroom, bathroom and TV area.

ABOVE Marion Russek spent a lot of time sourcing the ribbed plastic sheet to create the look of a genuine shipping container.

ABOVE The roof is made of corrugated packing material.

wall for a bed and bedside cabinet without either overlapping the window. It also helps to check whether the house looks correctly proportioned and that the ceilings are not too high.

At this stage, she plans all the electrics too, deciding where to put lamps and ceiling lights and assessing whether it will be possible to run wires invisibly from the power supply to each location.

Then comes the sourcing of the materials, which proved to be the biggest challenge on this project.

To give them extra strength, containers have a very particular ribbed structure. After a lot of research, Marion found some plastic sheeting in the right scale made by Plastruct that closely resembled the shape of the ribbing. The corrugated panelling for the roof turned out to be even more difficult to find, because she wanted sheeting with larger 'waves' than were readily available, but a friend in the packaging industry helped her out.

The basic structure was built using foam board. Marion then clad it with the various wall and roof sheeting that she had found. 'And the corners of the container – where they are hooked up – are something that I had to design myself and print in 3D,' she explained.

'A shipping container is not as easy to build as it would first appear.'

3D printing is a technique that Marion uses extensively to create chairs, taps, toilets and basins. Despite the convenience of being able to quickly print another version of an item that she has used before, she tends to create new ones each time. She admits that: 'I hate to make more than one of a kind.'

The windows were another major challenge, despite their deceptively simple shape. Like the cladding, they are made of plastic. In her previous projects, Marion had worked mainly with wood and foam board, so she had to learn how this new material behaves. They are fitted with Venetian blinds. 'It took me a long time to figure out how best to make these so that they look as real as possible,' she said.

LEFT A piece of modern art completes the contemporary decor.

3D printing

Additive manufacturing – more commonly known as 3D printing – allows you to create your own bespoke fixtures and fittings, especially when you cannot find them ready made.

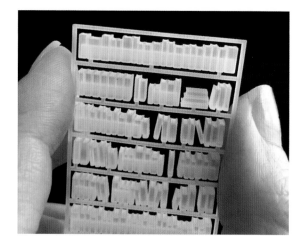

3D PRINTING IS THE PROCESS OF MAKING a physical object from a three-dimensional computerized drawing. It is increasingly being used to create building components such as pillars and columns. These would traditionally have been cast in resin. Instead of creating the master, building a mould and then casting each one individually, the object can be created as a digital design and printed multiple times and in different scales. 3D printing also works well for small items of furniture, particularly modern pieces such as basins that have a clean, angular outline.

BELOW This summerhouse cum reading room is a commercially available kit that has been 3D printed in 1:48 scale. *Maker: Carol Kubrican, True2Scale Miniatures*

ABOVE A shelf of 3D printed books.

BELOW 3D printed items can be easily painted with acrylics.
Credit: Carol Kubricon/True2Scale

The initial design is created in a 3D drawing package such as OpenSCAD or Sketchup. The latter was developed with backing from Google and thus is relatively easy and intuitive to use; this has quickly made it a popular choice for hobbyists taking their first steps in 3D design. However, it works best on a PC. If you have a Mac, then Cheetah3D is a good alternative and not excessively priced.

Achieving proficiency with even the most user-friendly of design packages takes time, so it is worth experimenting with the software to create a few objects on screen before investing in a 3D printer. There are a number of services that will print out designs from files – a bit like taking your holiday snaps in to be developed – so you can test how your design turns out. These include 4D Model Shop,

Blueprint Model Shop, Shapeways and 3D Print UK. Make an initial pencil sketch of the item you want to create before transferring it to the computer. This will give you a chance to think about the shape and scale of the item in detail before you have to worry about working with the software or how the object should be printed.

There is an extensive hobby community online that make their designs available for free, as long as they are for personal use. These can be printed as they are. Taking one of these designs as a starting point and customizing it can be a good way to help you get to grips with the software. There are particularly large numbers of designs available in 1:48 scale, as this is also the scale used by model railway enthusiasts working in O Gauge, many of whom are early adopters of 3D printing.

For those who lack confidence in their digital drawing skills, or are not keen to try their hand at 3D computerized design, there are other options. The first is to scan real-life objects using a 3D scanner. However, when scanning it is important to do this against a plain backdrop, otherwise the scanner may also pick up the background, causing interference to the design.

The scanners on the consumer market can only deal with objects of a certain size; a table or chair may be too large to scan effectively, so this is often only an option for ornaments.

Many public institutions are beginning to scan their exhibits and make the files available. They are keen to create a digital record of the object for cataloguing purposes; these files are of sufficiently high quality to create a life-sized copy of the object

BELOW 3D printing can be used to create even quite complex shapes, like this antler chandelier.
Maker: Marion Russek

for the museum if it were destroyed, so are more than adequate to create a scale version. The British Museum in the UK has a good online catalogue.

An alternative is to use photo manipulation software. Autodesk 123D Catch offers a free app for each of the major smartphone operating platforms. This stitches together a series of photographs to create a 3D model.

This technique has been used to successfully create a full-sized copy of the destroyed Arch of Palmyra, Syria. This was done using professional-grade software; the packages available on the consumer market are not quite to the same standard. But the software is constantly improving and is eminently good enough to create miniature objects.

PRINTING PROCESS

Once drawn, the object needs to be printed. You can send your designs to a professional print shop. They will check the files are suitable for printing and recommend how to fix files if they are not.

Until an object is prepared for printing, it is not possible to tell whether there are any aspects missing from the design that means it is not feasible to print. Nettfab is a free computer program that can be used to check design files for missing chunks and

BELOW The wicker chair in this bedroom has cleverly been created with 3D printing.
Maker: Marion Russek

to repair holes. If you decide to use an existing design for your early printing experiments produced by someone else, check whether it has been previously printed. It is best to see how well you get on with the design aspect – which is the more complicated part of the process – before spending too much money on hardware. Even though the cost of a 3D printer is coming down, using a printing service could save you money.

Once the file has been checked, it has to be translated into print-ready instructions, or G-code. The process is known as 'slicing'. The printed object is built up in layers and slicing software literally cuts the design into layers to establish what should be printed at each stage. Again, there is a range of software packages available, but printers are usually designed to work with a specific one, so it is important to use the one that is recommended by the manufacturer of whichever printer you buy.

The printer melts a roll of filament, extruding it gradually to build up the object. Different printers work with different types and thicknesses of filament. The most common are plastic, but cutting-edge printers can print in metal, while some have been designed to work with chocolate! Again, it is important to check which filament is recommended for your printer.

In the early days of 3D printing, the most common plastic filament was acrylonitrile butdiene styrene (ABS), but now polylactic acid (PLA) has taken over as the standard medium. PLA is a biodegradable substance derived from corn or maize; it has increased in popularity partly because of its improved environmental credentials. ABS also has a tendency to crack and warp if the printed object fails to cool evenly. Most printers now come with a heated print-bed that keeps the object at a constant temperature during printing and then allows it to cool gradually afterwards to reduce cracking.

PLA comes in a range of colours and is increasingly being mixed with wood fibre or brick dust to create a realistic effect. Wood-impregnated filament even smells like wood when gently sanded to smooth off any raw edges left by printing.

FINISHING AND PAINTING PRINTED PIECES

As with traditional computer printers, most 3D printers offer different levels of quality from draft to fine. This determines the thickness of each layer, which at its finest can be just 1 micron (0.01mm). However, as objects are built up in layers, you may still notice slight ridges on the finished article that need to be smoothed for the best result.

Some modellers use filler primer to fill in the dents. The object can also be smoothed by lightly rubbing it with acetone. This needs to be done with care. Acetone eliminates the ridges by re-melting the plastic; it is easy to be a bit too heavy-handed and create small holes, especially as the plastic

may not be as thick as you expect. To save on filament, printers build larger surface areas up using a honeycomb structure.

The printer may also build supports to give the object strength while it is being printed. These should be removed using a scalpel or side cutters, keeping sanding to a minimum. It is surprising how much heat can be generated by sanding – certainly enough to re-melt the plastic.

Once smooth, the object can be cleaned to remove any dirt and grease and then primed using a standard acrylic primer. This gives a good surface for painting with acrylics. The same process should be followed for cleaning and preparing any 3D printed items that you have bought.

BELOW All the items in this bakery shop display have been 3D printed at 1:48 scale.

COUNTRY LIFE

IT IS A STYLE MUCH LOVED BY interior designers, so it is hardly surprising that shabby chic has quickly made it to smaller scales, as more and more miniaturists decide to build cottages rather than grand houses.

A miniature cottage has many advantages. Like a room box, its generally smaller scale and limited number of rooms means the project takes up less display room in your full-sized house and may be quicker to complete. And unlike a big Georgian or Victorian dolls' house, it does not immediately imply the property should be decorated in a particular style. Many of us live in old workers' cottages today that have been updated to fit the needs of modern life.

A miniature cottage can be decorated in your own style, or at least the style you would choose if you lived in a country cottage and not a city centre apartment. And for many, it is the rustic look of shabby chic.

The combination of pastel shades and floral wallpaper and fabric with items of furniture that look well-used lends itself to the miniature property. The impact of strong colours and glossy paints is intensified in small places, so the rather dusty and faded palette of shabby chic can be easier to work with to create a naturalistic scene.

OPPOSITE Sue Kendell has made all the items in this cosy lounge from scratch with the exception of the lights and the plates in the dresser. She has used a mixture of 3D printing, laser cutting and traditional techniques to create the furniture.
Maker: Sue Kendell, Molly Sue Miniatures

It also provides a lot of scope for miniaturists to customize items. Some 25 years ago, in the early days of shabby chic, worn items were picked up for next to nothing in vintage fairs and flea markets. Now, much that appears to be tatty and well-loved has been made to look that way on purpose.

A lick of paint followed by some targeted sanding quickly makes a chair or table look like it has been knocked about over years of use. The same techniques are used in small scale and can quickly transform a manufactured item picked up in a dolls' house shop or online into a unique piece.

Shabby chic appeals to the miniaturist's love of upscaling. Secondhand furniture can be painted and renovated to give it a new lease of life. Broken items can be repurposed. Full-sized shops and cafés are awash with turn-of-the-century treadle sewing machine bases that have been turned into tables. Why not do the same in miniature?

But if all of this feels a little too mainstream and you really want to escape to the country, why not contemplate building a log cabin? Marion Russek's chalet would look perfectly at home on any remote tree-lined alpine slope. Karin Foster, on the other hand, has taken inspiration from the resilient people of rural America who did whatever they could to survive on the remote prairies during the Great Depression.

COTTAGES

RIGHT The veranda of this clapboard cottage would make an ideal place to settle down with a good book, or even to simply while away the hours watching the world go by.

Maker: Jodi Sophia Anderson

BELOW Emma Metcalf was inspired by the UK television series *Snowdonia 1890*, in which the presenters recreated life in a Victorian Welsh stone cottage. Starting with a basic cottage kit, she used ModRoc to create the rough stone walls and 'slate' window sills, while real slate was used for the flooring.

Maker: Emma Metcalf

LEFT Wisteria Cottage got its name after Jan Simpson Gilham perfected the way to make climbing plants and have them look as if they are gradually creeping across the porch roof. Kits from Templewood Miniatures were used to create the trailing ivy, hollyhocks and daisies and the tubs of flowers.
Maker: Jan Simpson Gilham

BELOW A specialist in miniature fireplaces, Chris Brooking recreates an English Tudor kitchen in a room box. The weathering techniques he learnt making military models have stood him in good stead, as the grate appears to be coated in the soot of countless open fires.
Maker: Chris Brooking, Firecraft Miniatures

ABOVE With its slate floors, big open grate and a collection of pottery on the dresser and hung over the mantelpiece, this kitchen room box suggests a rural rather than an urban setting.
Maker: Ingeborg Riesser

RIGHT A refurbished bargain bought from US classified advertising site Craig's List has become a desirable shabby chic cottage. An eclectic mix of floral fabrics and wallpapers has turned this room into a relaxed, but sophisticated bedroom.
Maker: Claudia Hill-Sparks

Shabby chic

Shabby chic is a style that is loved by interior decorators and miniature makers alike. It suggests that something has been loved and well used over many years – even when we know the piece of furniture is brand new and has been made to look that way on purpose. Vintage items have often been heavily painted and then knocked about with use, showing obviously time-worn areas. A few clever painting techniques can help you to get the look in minutes, rather than waiting for the effect to be generated through years of use.

DISTRESSING A PIECE OF FURNITURE

1 Paint the item with a rough coat of acrylic paint in a dark colour (grey or blue-grey work well) and leave to dry. The paint coverage does not need to be particularly even.

2 Paint the item with one or two more coats of acrylic paint, this time in your chosen colour for the top surface. Again, the coats do not need to be particularly even, as you will be rubbing the item down later to give it a distressed look. However, you do want it to cover the base layer sufficiently, so that the darker colour will only show on the sanded areas.

3 Sand the piece of furniture to give it a worn effect, paying attention to corners, edges and around any drawer or door handles. You want to reveal the colour underneath in some places, the base wood in others.

4 Varnish with a thin coat of acrylic varnish to seal the paint.

TIP: If your furniture has drawers, consider lining them with a piece of floral paper. The paper can be aged by gently rubbing with sandpaper and brushing it with a very thin coat of watered down brown acrylic. Alternatively, you can soak it in a little cold tea or coffee. Tea will give the paper a pinkish hue; coffee will make it appear browner. Be careful when you take the paper out of the liquid. It is prone to tearing until it has dried out again.

RIGHT Clever painting techniques can create the look of a well-loved piece.

RIGHT This washstand has been painted then coated in crackle glaze to create the cracked paint effect.

CRACKLE GLAZING FURNITURE

1 Paint the item with acrylic paint and leave to dry. You might want to choose a dark shade, as this coat will eventually be made to show through in places.

2 Coat the item with an even coat of crackle glaze medium and leave to dry.

3 Apply a thin, even coat of acrylic paint in a contrasting colour over the top. Try to keep brushing to a minimum. Leave to dry. The surface should crack as it dries.

4 Varnish with a thin coat of acrylic varnish to seal the paint.

TIP: The crackle glaze medium could also be applied to bare wood, covering the wood completely or just applying it in small areas to give a patchy worn look, and then painted over with acrylic paint.

LEFT This wash stand has been painted then coated in crackle glaze to create the cracked painted effect.
Maker: Petite Properties & Claire Wolfe

CREATING A FOXED MIRROR

LEFT This distressed settle looks like a piece of furniture that has seen many years of service.

1 If your frame is bright and shiny, tone it down with a thin wash of brown acrylic paint and leave to dry. Dry brush gold acrylic paint over the surface allowing a little brown paint to show through. Leave to dry.

2 Cut a piece of mirrored card slightly larger than the aperture of the frame. Mix up more watery brown acrylic paint and dip a toothbrush into it. Spatter paint the mirrored card by flicking the bristles of the brush over the card to create a fine spray of paint. Create a light coverage on a few areas with the occasional heavier patch. Practise on a piece of paper first. Leave to dry.

3 Glue the mirrored card into the frame.

RIGHT The aged effect is enhanced by rubbing down the edges and round the lock where a trunk would experience the most wear.

Chocolate-box cottage

A few key structural changes transformed an American-style kit house into the quintessential English country cottage.

CAROLINE DUPUIS' FIRST FORAY INTO miniatures was making architectural models in cardboard. Having made a few, she set up Cinderella Moments and started to sell her work. Commissions followed and before long, customers were asking her to leave the back off the property so that they could furnish the inside. But, unsure whether the paper constructions would be strong enough to support

RIGHT The bay window was replaced to make this kit look more authentically English on the outside.

BELOW Inside, soft tones and floral fabrics complete the look.

furniture, she began to build houses from kits, adapting them to meet customers' requirements, and then from scratch. 'I realized that I also loved decorating these little houses. I had a vision of how every little aspect should look, so I started learning how to make furniture. I was able to try out all of my decorating dreams in miniature,' Caroline said.

This Wiltshire Cottage started life as a 1:12 scale Westville kit by Greenleaf Dollhouses. The original looks quite typically colonial American, but removing the porch and the side bay window and changing the front bay window to a more English threepenny bit design transformed the cottage into something that looks more authentic. Covering the exterior in stones and bricks made from pre-mixed concrete completed the English picture postcard effect.

Caroline has made a range of different dolls' houses from French-style rooms to beach cottages, wedding chapels and artists' studios, though they all share a similar shabby-chic style. They have also

ABOVE The attic features a display of miniatures left over from other projects.

ABOVE Flowers trailing around the door complete the country cottage look.

RIGHT The lounge reflects the owner's 'whimsical sense of style'.

BELOW The range was copied from a vintage advert for a cooker made by US company GE.

tended not to feature a kitchen – either because it wasn't appropriate, or the model was too small. But the Wiltshire Cottage would not have been complete without one.

The heart of any cosy country kitchen is a range. Unable to find a stove of the right style, Caroline set about building one.

She found an advert from the 1950s for a pink cooker made by US company GE and used that as the basis for her miniature version. Inspired by the successful result, she added cabinets, shelves, table and a built-in pantry cupboard in the corner. In the end, only the chair was purchased; everything else was made. But this is what appeals to Caroline about the miniatures hobby: 'I love new challenges and projects, figuring out new ways to do things like the stove.'

Over the years, Caroline has amassed a range of miniatures that did not have a home – either things she had made that were left over from other projects, or gifts from friends. The Westville kit includes a small attic space. This proved the ideal place to display an eclectic assortment of items and give personality to the property.

'I imagine a single girl living in the house. She's a crafty gal with a whimsical sense of style, somebody very romantic who likes old things, to which she can give a new life.'

Thatching roofs

Nothing can do more to create that traditional chocolate box cottage than adding a thatched roof. As with the full-scale version, this is not a quick process, because the thatch must be attached in sections. However, with a little time and patience, it is possible to turn your cottage into a classic country retreat.

TRADITIONAL THATCHING

1 The usual material for thatching a dolls' house is coir, which is fibre from the coconut husk. It can be purchased in full length bundles (9²⁷⁄₃₂in (250mm)) or in trimmed bundles (7³¹⁄₆₄in (190mm)). Dolls' house suppliers typically sell the trimmed bundles. A spray adhesive, or PVA glue, is the recommended glue to use. Cut thick card or mounting board panels to fit the size of your roof. These will be glued to the existing base once the thatching has been completed. Check that the panels are a good fit for the house. They should be slightly loose, because they will become thicker with the addition of thatch. Once the thatch is complete, it is very difficult to trim the roof panel.

2 Measure ¹⁹⁄₃₂in (15mm) up from the bottom of the panel and draw a line horizontally.

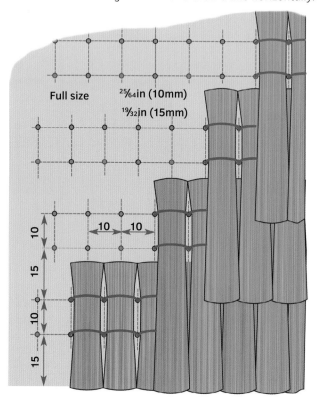

Full size ²⁵⁄₆₄in (10mm) ¹⁹⁄₃₂in (15mm)

Then draw another ²⁵⁄₆₄in (10mm) up from that. Keep drawing parallel lines across the roof panel, alternating the spacing (see spacing diagram), finishing off with a ²⁵⁄₆₄in (10mm) gap at the top. Do not worry if you have a little bit of unmarked roof still left at the top of the panel, this piece will be covered with the roof stitching. On each of the ²⁵⁄₆₄in (10mm) gaps, measure vertical lines ²⁵⁄₆₄in (10mm) apart. Each new row should be offset from the last by ¹³⁄₆₄in (5mm) to create a brick pattern. This ensures that the bundles of coir will fit neatly between the bundles on the previous row and cover any gaps.

3 Tape the two roof panels back to back. Make holes at the corners of the ²⁵⁄₆₄in (10mm) squares through both panels. A compass point or an awl work well. Alternatively a fine nail may also be used. Once all the holes are made, separate the panels.

4 Cut the coir to length. The majority of the bundles will need to be cut to 2³¹⁄₆₄in (63mm) in length, but you will need enough cut to a length of 1¹⁹⁄₆₄in (33mm) to do the first row on each side of the roof. The bundles for the ridge course need to be cut to 4⁵⁹⁄₆₄in (125mm) and set aside until you are ready to make the ridge panel. A cardboard cradle is useful for keeping the cut fibres straight and together. Line the cradle with a piece of paper before beginning to put the fibres into it. Once you have a sizeable bundle, the paper can be wrapped the full way around and taped together, making a neat bundle that can be kept until you are ready.

5 Starting at the eaves (bottom of the panel), use a bodkin or darning needle to sew sections of the 1¹⁹⁄₆₄in (33mm) long coir into place. The sections should be about

the thickness of a pencil. The bundles should be placed so that the top is ¹³⁄₆₄in (5mm) below the next row of holes and the ends extend slightly beyond the edge of the roof panel. At this stage you can use any colour thread (the stitches will be covered by the bundles of coir in the next row). There is no set pattern for the stitches, but two horizontal lines of stitching work well and hold the bundles firm (see below).

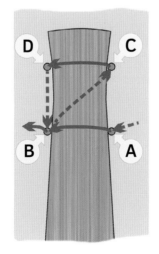

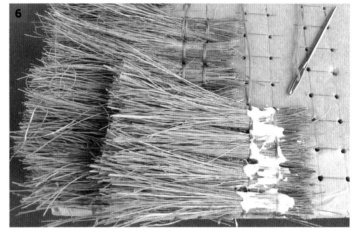

6 Once the first row (the eaves course) has been complete, spread PVA glue over the stitched ends of the bundles. Then begin the second row (the brow course) using the 2³¹⁄₆₄in (63mm) long fibres. These should start just below the third set of holes and completely cover the eaves course. Continue to lock the stitches with glue. Do not be tempted to pull out any stray fibres, as this may loosen the whole bundle; simply trim with scissors. Continue working in rows until you have reached

the top. Repeat steps 5 and 6 for the second panel. Once both panels are complete, they can be fitted to the house. You will need to use plenty of PVA. Tape or a few dressmaking pins pushed in are also useful to hold the panels temporarily in place while the glue dries. There will be a gap at the top of up to ²⁵⁄₃₂in (20mm) with no thatch. Cut two strips of mounting board the thickness of the thatch and glue them on. This will pad it out to the thickness of the thatch. It will be covered by the ridge course.

7 Measure a piece of thick card or mounting board that is 3$\frac{35}{64}$in (90mm) wide and as long as the ridge line of the roof of your house. Score the card down the centre on the reverse and fold to make an apex. Cover the right side of the panel with brown paper or paint it in as close a colour match to the coir as possible. This is so any gaps between the bundles do not show. Measure $\frac{25}{64}$in (10mm) from the bottom edge on each side and draw a line, followed by two further lines $\frac{25}{64}$in (10mm) apart. Then mark these into $\frac{25}{64}$in (10mm) squares and make holes in the corners as before.

8 Using the 4$\frac{59}{64}$in (125mm) bundles, sew these over the ridge panel. The middle of the bundle should be at the apex of the panel, such that the ends hang off both sides.

Do not be tempted to glue the bundles, as they need to be able to move and flex slightly when you fold and attach the panel to the house. Use dark reddish brown polyester thread to create a criss-cross pattern (see below); a final straight line of stitches through the top set of holes makes a neat edge. The stitches are designed to show as on a real thatched roof. Gently bend the card,

trimming the fibres if necessary to create a neat edge, and glue the panel into place. Again, dressmaking pins will hold the panel in place while the glue dries. PVA glue can now be brushed over the ridge fibres to lock them into place. The thatch at the end of the panels may also need to be

coated to hold them in place when you slide the full roof assembly in between the side walls.

TIP: It may be necessary to use half bundles at the end of each course to stop the panels from becoming too thick.

Full size
$\frac{25}{64}$in (10mm)
1$\frac{49}{64}$in (45mm)

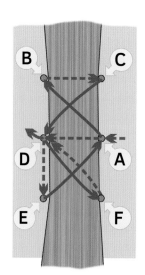

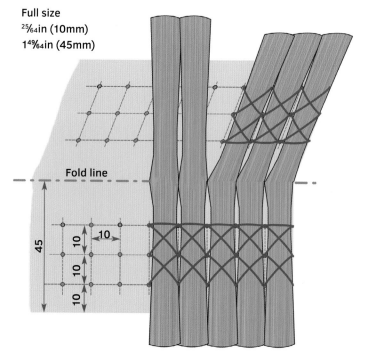

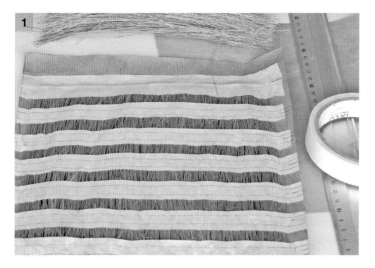

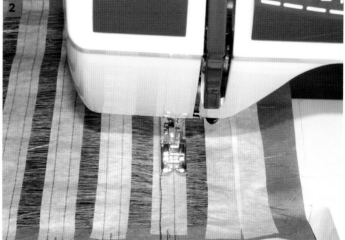

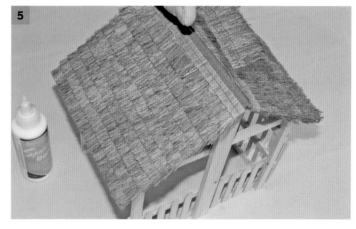

STRIP THATCHING

1 Spread uncut coir fibre out evenly on brown paper. It should be about ⅛in (3mm) thick. Tape the ends of the fibre down using ²⁵/₃₂in (20mm) masking tape and then apply rows of tape ²⁵/₆₄in (10mm) apart.

2 Using a sewing machine, sew two lines over each row of tape ⁵/₁₆in (8mm) apart.

3 Cut the thatch into strips, cutting just along the edge of the tape so that the first strip is ²⁵/₃₂in (20mm) wide and all other strips are 1³/₁₆in (30mm) wide. Remove most of the brown paper, leaving a thin strip where it has been sewn to the coir and masking tape. Stick the strips to the roof with the masking tape side down. Overlap each strip so that you do not see any tape.

4 For the ridge, spread lengths of coir 2in (50mm) long over brown paper and tape the ends and the middle as above, leaving a gap of ¹³/₆₄in (5mm) between the rows of tape. Sew two lines of stitches. You can use a bright colour, or zigzag stitches for effect. Do not sew through the tape.

5 Remove the tape and stick the sewn strip to the centre section of the roof. This time, the strip should be brown paper side down.

ALTERNATIVES

If you do not feel confident sewing coir into place, you could consider using a number of other materials. A piece of 'cut pile' towelling (not terry towelling) painted an appropriate shade, or fur fabric glued on to the roof can look quite effective, especially on smaller roofs. If choosing fur, avoid the 'curly' fur that is sold for making some soft toys. Fur fabric also tends to be quite fine, so will need spraying with hairspray and combing to ensure the pile lays straight.

BARNS AND LOG CABINS

RIGHT Set in the US at the time of the Great Depression, this cabin evokes what people would have done to get by – growing their own vegetables and selling any surplus to make ends meet. It took several goes to paint the house with glue then acrylic and a lot of sanding to get the desired peeling paint effect, suggesting the residents are truly on their uppers.
Maker: Karin Foster

BELOW The owner of this cabin has clearly been inspired by the magnificence of the scenery outside and has turned his retreat into an artist's studio with good natural light in which to paint.
Maker: Robert Off

ABOVE The artist's studio is filled with postcards featuring Amy Gross's favourite works of art, as well as miniature versions of her own artworks and invitations for the exhibitions where her work has been featured. *Maker: Amy Gross*

BELOW As with many a real-life barn conversion, there is a double-height ceiling. A walkway allows access to the first floor, while the spiral staircase leads to the eaves. *Maker: Lauren Hicks and Adam Fray*

ABOVE Based on a kit by Real Good Toys, this barn is advertised as a typical farm building featuring stalls for horses and other animals. However, Amy Gross converted it in the way she would have been keen to do in real life were she to have a big enough budget. It has a café downstairs that would be run by her mother and her own artist's studio upstairs.. *Maker: Amy Gross*

BELOW Built from scratch in just four weeks to meet the deadline for a dolls' house competition, this barn was inspired by a ruined, brick hay barn in Warwickshire. The makers added elements from an old Suffolk cottage and a converted print works in the London district of Borough, UK to create their vision for their dream property. *Maker: Lauren Hicks and Adam Fray*

Miniature mountain retreat

This Alpine retreat is the perfect place to curl up in front of a log fire with a hot chocolate and a good book after a day spent walking or skiing in the mountains.

HAVING TALKED FOR YEARS ABOUT buying an alpine chalet as a holiday home, Marion Russek eventually decided that the maintenance of a full-sized property would be too much hassle and the answer was to build one in miniature. She had made various dolls' houses as a child and also completed a Glenwood kit as an adult, so she felt confident enough to tackle a scratch-build.

Marion took to Pinterest for inspiration, but also made a trip to Bregenzerwald in Austria, which she describes as 'the hub for wood buildings, modern and traditional'. The research trip was particularly valuable as she learned more about the construction methods used to create alpine cabins – knowledge she translated into design drawings using Live Interior 3D software followed by a 1:100 scale model in foam board.

This revealed that the four-bedroom house she originally conceived was far too big for a weekend retreat and needed to be scaled down to a more modest two bedrooms. Based on the model, she also decided that she did not want to have an opening side – as in many traditional houses – because it would prevent her from placing furniture in the downstairs rooms against all four walls. But it was clearly crucial to be able to see inside the cabin. The solution was to create a property where the top floor lifts off entirely.

The cabin is made of ²⁵⁄₆₄in (10mm) thick foam board, with grooves cut to imitate beams. Marion initially attempted to build the cabin from balsa wood and dowels, but found it difficult to get a consistent size and finish. The foam board is covered in structured paper and four or five coats of acrylic paint to give the impression of wood.

'I always had a soft spot for antler chandeliers,' Marion commented, but the best way to fit ceiling lights when the top storey lifts off required some

ABOVE The cabin has been covered in textured paper to give the impression of wood.

BELOW The bedroom is spacious enough for two beds.

thought. In the end, the wiring had to be integrated into the ceiling beams. She also tried several ways to make the chandelier herself before eventually finding a 3D printing file online that could be adapted to achieve the right look.

The dining chairs and the wicker chair upstairs were also printed in plastic. 3D printing allowed Marion to source the designs she wanted in whatever scale and then reduce them to 1:12 scale. Like many other dolls' house enthusiasts, she now makes these files available via the online 3D printing service Shapeways.

ABOVE The pedestal has been made from a log, continuing the rustic theme throughout.

LEFT AND BELOW Lots of cushions complete the feel of a snug mountain hideaway.

'The solution was to create a property where the top floor lifts off entirely.'

BELOW The bedroom includes a desk area.

Fireplaces and flicker units

Nothing is more inviting on a cold winter's evening than the warm glow of an open fire. That goes for dolls' houses just as much as it does for full-sized homes.

MINIATURE FIREPLACES ARE COMMONLY supplied with a bulb and a resin insert shaped to look like a pile of coals to achieve just such a warm glow. Predominantly black, the insert is translucent red in places, allowing the light from the bulb to shine through. The bulbs are wired to the power supply in the same way as you would connect ceiling and wall lights (see Lighting and wiring, pages 128–129). The only thing you need to remember if you are fitting bulbs into your fireplaces is to add the position of the fires to any wiring plan you make and to include the number of lit grates to your tally of bulbs, so that you can choose the correct power supply.

DANCING FLAMES

Miniaturists are increasingly taking things a step further, installing a flicker unit with the fire to give the impression of dancing flames. Flicker units are small electronic circuits that adjust the brightness of the bulb. A random timing generator controls how long the bulb stays at different brightness levels so it appears to flicker erratically.

Each flicker unit has an input and an output. The input is wired to your power supply and the output to the bulb in the fireplace. Multiple fires can be wired to the same unit; a unit with two outputs can operate up to 20 bulbs, though check the rating of the individual unit you buy to be sure that it can safely power the number of fires you have in your house.

Avoid wiring neighbouring rooms to the same output if you can. There is nothing unsafe about having adjoining rooms on the same circuit – it is simply that they will flicker in unison. The flicker

RIGHT Adding a flicker unit can make the 'flames' appear to dance randomly.

unit applies the same brightness setting to all the bulbs that are connected to an output. This is evident if both fires are side by side, but less so if the two fires controlled by the one output are at different corners of the house.

Each flicker unit has a number of speed settings allowing the user to control how quickly or slowly the setting changes. The speed chosen is very much a personal thing and you will need to experiment with the units once they are installed to see what you prefer.

If you are modelling an older property, such as a Tudor or Georgian house, and you have candles or oil lamps instead of electric lights, you might like to experiment with wiring some of the candlesticks to the flicker unit. This will give the impression that the candle has been placed in a draughty room and may be extinguished at any point.

ABOVE AND RIGHT
Fireplaces are usually supplied with a resin insert, which when lit from behind appears to glow like the embers of a fire.

ADDING SMOKE

If you want to have smoking chimneys, this is feasible using off-the-shelf smoke generators that have been developed for model railways. They are small electrically powered units that heat a specially formulated oil to give off smoke. The most commonly used generators are manufactured by Seuthe. They come in a range of different shapes and sizes, but the number 6 that is designed for O Gauge and Gauge 1 trains is best for dolls' houses.

The units need an opening at the top of the chimney of ²⁵⁄₆₄in (10mm) to let the smoke out, so can be fitted inside most 1:12 scale chimney pots and some 1:24 pots. At the smaller scale, care must be given to ensuring there is a sufficient outlet at the top and that there is some clearance around the unit when the chimney pot is slotted over it. The units become hot after a period of use; they make the smoke by heating and burning the oil. So make sure there is clearance around the unit to ensure that the heat generated can dissipate. For this reason, it is best to fit them within traditional terracotta chimney pots; plastic has a tendency to warp or become misshapen if exposed to heat.

The base of the unit can be fitted into the chimney stack to hold it securely; take care to recess it only as far as is necessary for it to be fixed firmly. Most of the unit should sit proud of the stack, because the pot slides over to conceal it. Again, embedding it in a wooden stack is best because of the heat generated. Metal sheathing can be used to support the smoke generator and create a barrier between the unit and the chimney stack, but plastic should be avoided. The top of the pot should just conceal the unit, again to ensure that the outlet for the smoke is as unrestricted as possible.

It is worth leaving the chimney pots unsecured. This allows them to be removed, giving easy access to the smoke generator for refilling. The oil is injected into the top of the unit with a syringe. It can be a bit tricky, so it is useful to be able to see what you are doing. The oil can stain or mark painted finishes if spilled, so you want to minimize the chance of that happening.

It is not necessary to fit smoke generators in every chimney. The units are not cheap, so the costs can quickly mount up if you have multiple chimneys on a stack; even relatively small Victorian houses could have five or six chimney pots on the roof. It also looks more realistic to limit the number; it is unlikely that you would have a fire burning in every grate in the house simultaneously and, therefore, smoke rising from every chimney.

LEFT The smoke units can be easily embedded in the chimney stack.

RIGHT The smoke units burn a special oil, which you can top up using a syringe.

Having only a few on each stack creates additional distance between smoking chimneys and helps any heat to dissipate. Each also needs power to operate, so by controlling the number of units you contain the power requirements and avoid overloading the power supply.

ABOVE Smoke gently billows from the chimneys.

WIRING THE UNITS

Each smoke generator is fitted with a pair of wire tails. These tend to be quite short, because the units are designed for use in model trains where the distances from power supply to unit are limited.

You will need to run two wires from your power supply up to the roof, finding the best route to get them up through the centre of the chimney stack while remaining concealed. You will want to do this before you tile the roof and decorate the upper floors.

The wires should be quite flexible, because you will want to join them to the tails of the unit and then conceal the excess in the chimney stack before pushing the units gently into the holes you have made for them.

It does not matter which way round the wires are connected, but the usual convention is to connect the brown wire to the positive. The wires will need to be twisted together or joined using solder and the joint covered by electrical tape or shrink wrap. There is little room within the chimney stack to accommodate any form of connector. However, once the wires have been joined and the unit firmly seated within the stack, it is unlikely that the joints will be disturbed, so they should hold perfectly firmly.

CONNECTING TO THE POWER SUPPLY

Most of the commercially available smoke generators are rated at 14–16 volts and will work on AC or DC power. However, they will work perfectly satisfactorily on a typical 12V circuit; the units will simply produce slightly less smoke – a gentle billowing drift, rather than the great plumes you would expect of a train in full steam. You do not, however, want to use a smoke generator that is rated at less than 12V. This will run too intensively and burn out prematurely.

The units draw around 0.3A (300mA) – equivalent to 6–8 light bulbs. As a result, it is important to ensure that your power supply has sufficient capacity to take the extra load.

You could consider connecting the smoke generators to their own discrete circuit with a separate power supply. This means you do not have to worry about the difference between the voltage used for the smoke units and the lights. It also allows you to decide on the power supply that you need just for the smoke generators and ensure that it has a sufficient rating in amps. Finally, you can then switch off the smoke generators separately. If you link the generators and the lights to the same circuit, you will need to fit a switch, to be able to turn off the smoke generators separately from the lights.

It is inadvisable to leave the smoke generators running the entire time. If they burn the available supply of oil and run dry, then they can quickly overheat causing them to burn out prematurely. But if operated in line with the manufacturer's instruction they are perfectly safe and will give hours of enjoyment.

GREAT OUTDOORS

EVERY DES RES COMES WITH A BIT of outside space, so it is unsurprising that many miniaturists are keen to add a garden to their dolls' house, or at the very least some window boxes, pots and planters.

But gardens do not have to butt up against a dolls' house. In fact, it can often be impossible to have an attached garden. No one wants to knock the heads off their miniature roses when they open the front of their dolls' house to reveal all the interior rooms.

This has led to some creative solutions. A modern property could be enhanced by a roof garden, while some hobbyists also choose to build gardens into the stand underneath their house. This has two key advantages. The garden does not require any more space; it is contained within the footprint of the existing dolls' house. It can also be put away, keeping it free of dust.

Increasingly gardens are being created as standalone scenes in their own right – and ones that require as many props and accessories as any dolls' house room. The starting point is usually a simple baseboard, such as a piece of MDF or plywood, with hedges, walls or fences that mark the edge of the garden. A room box with the top removed will serve just as well.

OPPOSITE Creating an English country cottage garden which reflected the one in Elizabeth Goudge's *Green Dolphin Street*, but also comprised plants that all flowered at the same time, proved a particular challenge when creating this cottage.
Maker: Elizabeth Slinn

Then – as with designing a full-sized garden – the important thing is to bring form and structure to the scene, with the addition of paths and flowerbeds. From greenhouses, gazebos and aviaries to sheds and the outdoor privy, there is a whole range of garden buildings that could be added to create a focal point – not to mention features like ponds and fountains. However, for some miniaturists, it is the garden building itself that is the draw. A conservatory kit, or even a glass terrarium of the kind available in many florists and garden centres, is a delightful and self-contained project.

There are as many types of miniature plant as you would find at the best of garden centres that can be used to fill a garden or conservatory. The challenge is to resist often quite beautiful miniatures to source a collection of flowers that genuinely would be in bloom at the same point in the year.

Gardens also offer the opportunity to incorporate animals – from the friendly hedgehog to the nesting blue tit, or Mel Jones' cat Thomas, who is stuck up a tree for eternity.

As with the houses to which the gardens relate, styles vary quite substantially. In this chapter, there are examples of the country cottage garden and the Mediterranean terrace, as well as Emma Waddell's more formal and geometric garden designs.

SHEDS AND GARDENS

LEFT A room box has been customized to make this walled garden scene. *Maker: Julie Campbell/ Bella Belle Dolls*

BELOW Conifers and lupins grow in this well-tended garden. In the background, a well-equipped greenhouse provides space to tend young plants. *Maker: Emma Waddell*

RIGHT A Mediterranean-inspired terrace is the perfect place to relax over a glass of wine on long, hot summer evenings. *Maker: Natures Soul Miniatures*

ABOVE Encompassed by a red brick wall, this garden has really been made to feel like an extension of the cottage. Blue tits feed on coconuts hung from the cherry tree, while Thomas, the cat, dangles precariously from a high branch.
Maker: Mel Jones

RIGHT A grand conservatory overlooks a formal garden that makes a central feature of the pond and fountain.
Maker: Emma Waddell

Water

If you want to give the impression of water in your dolls' house or miniature garden, you will need to use resin. The type varies depending on the effect that you are trying to create. The most important thing to decide is what effect you want and then select the right product for the job. Some resins set hard and crystal clear, making them ideal for creating ponds or puddles; others are softer and can easily be coloured and are better suited to making bubbles or suggesting a splashing fountain. It takes a little practice, but after a few goes, resin can be made to look like real water.

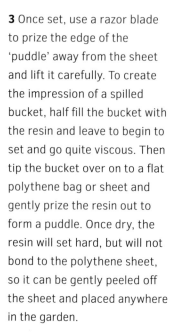

PUDDLES

1 Mix the resin and hardener together according to the pack instructions. You will need to measure carefully (see tips on moulding, pages 50–51).

2 Pour the mixture on to a clear plastic styrene sheet and put it in a warm, flat place to set for 24 hours. Try to shield it from dust to ensure it remains clear.

3 Once set, use a razor blade to prize the edge of the 'puddle' away from the sheet and lift it carefully. To create the impression of a spilled bucket, half fill the bucket with the resin and leave to begin to set and go quite viscous. Then tip the bucket over on to a flat polythene bag or sheet and gently prize the resin out to form a puddle. Once dry, the resin will set hard, but will not bond to the polythene sheet, so it can be gently peeled off the sheet and placed anywhere in the garden.

FOUNTAINS

This project describes how to make a fountain and pond full of fish, but could also apply to a sink full of washing up. You can fill any vessel you want provided it does not leak! If it has a hole in it, it will need to be sealed first with a small amount of epoxy resin. This should be invisible under the water.

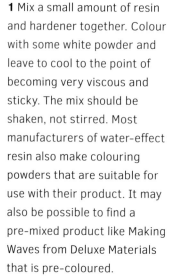

1 Mix a small amount of resin and hardener together. Colour with some white powder and leave to cool to the point of becoming very viscous and sticky. The mix should be shaken, not stirred. Most manufacturers of water-effect resin also make colouring powders that are suitable for use with their product. It may also be possible to find a pre-mixed product like Making Waves from Deluxe Materials that is pre-coloured.

2 Use a length of wire to tease out the resin mix and see how well it holds its shape. It should create a continuous stream (not drips) when dispensed slowly from the tip. You will need to experiment with how long it takes for the resin to get to this stage, but some makes might take a few hours to reach the right condition. A hot air gun is useful for speeding up the hardening process, but also for warming hardened resin to shape and mould it.

3 Attach the viscous resin to the spout of the fountain and drag it down to the bottom, at the same time extruding more. This is a bit fiddly, but ideally you want to stretch the flow out so that if it becomes any thinner, the strand of resin would break. Roughly, attach the end of the stream to the base of the pond, so that it appears to be splashing against the base.

4 Add additional threads alongside the first one to give the effect of flowing water. You may want some of the threads to peter out halfway down to make the stream appear wider at the top than the bottom.

5 Fix the fish in place in the basin of the fountain with tacky wax. This will avoid them moving when you add the water. Mix together some more resin and hardener as above. Fill the basin with the mixture using a syringe. Applying a clear mix over the turbulent base of the stream you have just created will give the impression of fast water breaking through stiller water. Fill the basin most of the way to the top and then leave to cool.

6 Colour the remaining resin with some white powder. After shaking, blow air into the mix using a syringe. This will make it aerated and bubbly. Spread this mixture on to the surface of the water in the pond. The resin in the pond should be still soft and 'molten'. This will allow the two preparations to blend slightly and give the effect of bubbles on the surface.

TIP: You can add resin to taps dripping into an empty sink. After setting firm you can add a 'puddle' of resin (see above) to give the impression of the water running across the base of the sink.

CONSERVATORIES

RIGHT This fully lit room box is about the same size as a paperback book. However, it still manages to evoke the great public conservatories of the Victorian era in the UK, such as Kew Gardens, London or the Royal Botanic Garden Edinburgh, not to mention hinting at an entire back-story of a secret rendezvous.
Maker: Aidan Campbell

BELOW You do not need to have a garden to have a fountain. Surrounded by potted ferns, the fountain is a lovely feature in this conservatory. Sit back, relax and enjoy the sound of cascading water.
Maker: Jo Medvenics

ABOVE A love of painting and revamping old furniture – be it family heirlooms or junkshop finds – led Christine-Léa Frisoni to develop a chic country style that here she extends to the conservatory and potting shed.
Maker: Christine-Léa Frisoni

RIGHT This conservatory replete with orchids, lilies and a fruiting grapevine is the ideal spot for pre-dinner cocktails.
Maker: Caroline Hamilton

Plants

Flowers work well in any setting from cottage gardens to florist shops or grand drawing rooms. All flowers are made in a similar way, building up layers of petals to create a more or less full bloom. The instructions below are for multi-layered peonies, but follow the same approach for any flower from azaleas to wisterias.

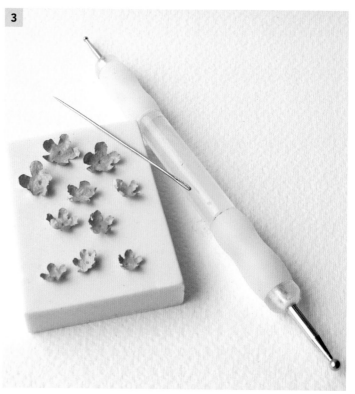

1 Paint several small sheets of tissue paper on both sides in slightly varying shades. Put out a little of each paint shade, but do not mix together completely. Moisten a flat brush slightly and paint roughly, adding tiny amounts of extra water if needed to make the paint flow. This method will result in naturalistic colour variation. Allow the paint to dry.

2 Use a petal punch to cut out shapes. You will need a punch that cuts five-petal shapes ⁹⁄₃₂in (7mm) across, one making ²⁵⁄₆₄in (10mm) flowers and a third cutting ¹⁵⁄₃₂in (12mm) shapes. You will need two of the smallest shapes, three of the medium and two of the largest shapes for each peony.

3 Lay the flower shapes on an eraser or petal-shaping pad and make a hole in the centre of each using a darning needle. Centre the hole as accurately as you can. If the hole is off-centre the petals will not arrange themselves evenly. Shape each petal by pressing gently with an embossing tool. This will curve them upwards and inwards and will give the edges a slightly frilly appearance. You may need to open up the holes again afterwards.

4 Cut lengths of wire up to 1⅝–2in (40–50mm) long. Dip the end of each wire into some glue, then slide a bead on to the tip. Leave to dry completely. Trim off any extra wire. Put a small quantity of yellow flower sprinkles into a bowl. Dip the top of the bead in glue, then in the flower sprinkles. When the glue is dry and the sprinkles are fixed firmly, you can trim them to a neat, round shape if needed.

5 Smear the bead lightly with glue below the sprinkles, then slide one of the small flower shapes up the stem. Gently roll it with your fingertips around the bead to cover the area below the stamens and leave to dry. Repeat with the second small shape, this time only smearing glue around the lower half of the bead and fixing the petals so they remain slightly open at the top. Move on to the three medium shapes and fix these with a dot of glue under the flower head, then the two

largest shapes. With each layer, arrange them so the petals are offset.

6 Punch five-petal shapes from green paper and fix one under each flower, shaping them so they curve slightly downwards. Punch out leaves from green paper with a Japanese maple punch. Run a darning needle along the length of each leaf to indicate a central vein and also to shape the leaf. Glue a leaf or two under some of the flowers or down some of the flower stems. Tidy up any glue marks with a dab of coloured paint.

You can make trees in the same way by creating five or six bundles containing around 30 fine copper wires twisted together along half their length. Then twist the bundles together at one end to form a thick trunk, while the untwisted copper filaments can be bent and shaped to form branches to which you can stick leaves and blossoms.

ON THE COAST

FOR GENERATIONS, WE HAVE LIVED by the coast, fishing, trading and occasionally getting involved in a little smuggling. Even now that most people live in cities, we flock to the seaside at the first hint of summer. It is only natural that this love of the sea would be translated into miniature. And in the case of Nell Corkin's 1:144 scale beach hut into a very small scale indeed.

A beach hut makes a great project on its own or as part of a wider beach scene – one that can be decorated in a wide range of styles. Some real-life beach hut owners simply use them as a place to change before a bracing swim in the sea; others use them as miniature holiday homes, even adding a gallery bed in the roof space. Similarly, they have been a seaside feature for over 150 years, since Victorian ladies first adopted the bathing machine as a way to get from the beach to the sea without being seen in their swimming costume. This means you have as wide a choice of periods to model as with any other style of building.

There is also a lot of scope for finding accessories outside of the usual world of dolls' house supplies. Seaside shops particularly sell a range of nauticalia that can be re-purposed for a coastal property. I have

OPPOSITE Brae Oktober combined a love of miniatures and lighthouses to create this stunning beacon inspired by the Chicago Harbor Light.
Maker: Brae Oktober

seen miniature ships' wheels, life rings, lanterns and even old-fashioned divers' helmets attached to the end of a keyring that could easily look at home in a beach hut or lighthouse.

Joanne Schmidt turned a collection of fossils and decorative minerals picked up in seaside gift shops into a geology museum, inspired by the one on the seafront at Lyme Regis, UK. Located on the Jurassic heritage coast, the museum is packed with ammonites and dinosaur fossils. Joanne's window display hints at the wealth of exhibits inside, but it is the pesky seagulls taking people's chips that really steal the show.

Brae Oktober showed herself to be an expert at re-purposing items for her lighthouse. Christmas decorations, hair rollers and coffee creamer containers all found their way into her model of the Chicago Harbor Light.

A coastal property makes a great first foray into the art of weathering. Many dolls' houses are pristine, but a beach hut or lighthouse does not look quite right without some signs of wear. These properties take a lot of battering from the elements, while the constant ebb and flow of the tide leaves a residue of seaweed and algae at the base.

BEACH HOUSES

RIGHT This beach hut is modelled in 1:144 scale but, despite its tiny size, it is packed with authentic seaside details.
Maker: Nell Corkin

ABOVE Herring gulls take advantage of human untidiness outside this model of a fossil museum and heritage centre, inspired by the Lyme Regis Museum on England's south coast and Tracy Chevalier's novel *Remarkable Creatures*. Real geological specimens are on display in the windows to entice visitors inside.
Maker: Joanne Schmidt

ABOVE A reed placemat was the inspiration for this beach house. It was eventually transformed into the roll-up blinds for the windows. A second bamboo placemat was turned into a rug.
Maker: Grazhina Kayhart

LEFT Built from scratch, this one-room beach hut is built on stilts and has upward swinging shutters like those near Grazhina Kayhart's home in Maine, USA.
Maker: Grazhina Kayhart

Using sound

Dolls' houses do not just need to be a visual delight. Why not evoke the general hustle and bustle of domestic life with the addition of sound? You could add a ringing doorbell or telephone, generate the sound of lapping waves and seagull cries, or have the radio playing in the kitchen. The possibilities are endless and effective results are achievable with a few readily available components.

PLACING YOUR SPEAKER

Sound has been used for some time by boat, plane and railway modellers. As a result there are a range of small speakers available that can be installed in the house. These can vary in cost, with some of the smallest being more expensive. The first step is to decide where you want to place the speaker to allow you to decide how small a speaker you need to use.

A speaker measuring $^{25}\!/_{32}$ x 1 $^{37}\!/_{64}$in (20 x 40mm) could easily be concealed within a chimney breast and provide quite impressive sound quality. Victorian doorbells were often mounted on a rectangular box or panel, which could be adapted to house a speaker. If you are modelling a newer style property, you could make rectangular boxes that look like hi-fi speakers and fit the genuine speaker inside.

There will be two wires coming from the speaker – a positive and a negative. You will need to run these from the speaker location to wherever you have chosen to mount the sound source. This will typically be at the back or underneath the house.

A small MP3 player, such as an Apple iPod, makes an ideal sound source. It is easy to transfer music and other sound effects on to the iPod. They are also small enough that they can easily be concealed below the house, or maybe even in a piece of dolls' house furniture such as a chest or bench seat.

It may be necessary to lengthen the wires to do this, but that can be easily achieved by soldering on an additional length of wire or joining the two with a chocolate block or crimp connector.

RIGHT An iPod hidden under the house can become the source of many different styles of music.

CONNECTING YOUR SPEAKER

The easiest way to connect your speaker to a sound source is by means of a jack plug. They are the thin, pointed connectors found on the end of a pair of headphones that plug into an iPod. There are two types: mono and stereo. There is no need to buy a stereo plug as you are connecting to a single speaker and will not be using stereo sound. However, most modern MP3 players are designed to work with stereo, so will work more reliably when connected via a stereo jack plug. Mono jack plugs have two inputs, known as the tip and the sleeve; stereo jack plugs have a third input – the ring. In both cases, the positive wire should be connected to the tip, the negative to the sleeve.

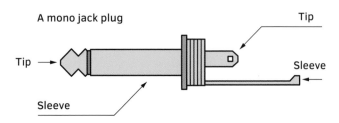

A mono jack plug

Tip →   Tip

                         Sleeve ←

Sleeve

– plays back the recording. This can be used to record a discrete sound, such as a doorbell or Victorian servants' bells. As they are integrated units, you will need to place them somewhere where you can easily access the button to press it. Alternatively, you can connect them to your concealed speaker, so that the 'growler unit' can be mounted somewhere else. This will require some soldering and, depending on the location of the unit, you may need to connect an additional push button which can be mounted somewhere more accessible.

TIP: Wireless speakers are becoming smaller and cheaper and make a great alternative if you do not want to try your hand at wiring. These connect to a smartphone using Bluetooth, allowing you to beam music and sound from your phone straight into your house.

Once connected the speaker can be plugged straight into your iPod. You can now spend your time sourcing the music and sound effects that you want to emanate from your house. If you decide to record some chatter to give the impression of people going about their business in the house, make sure that this is a relatively long recording. If the recording is too short and repeats regularly, this will be quite obvious. Music, on the other hand, could be in quite short bursts. Imagine a person practising a new piece on the piano; they may go over the same section again and again until they have perfected it.

OTHER SOUND SOURCES

While an iPod is a relatively easy thing to connect, the more adventurous maker may want to experiment with other sound sources. Model boat companies make a range of sound modules that come supplied with pre-recorded sound effects, such as boat engine noise and seagulls. These can be reprogrammed using the software supplied to generate any other domestic sounds you choose, such as chatter or a barking dog.

Toy stores, where you can build your own teddy bear or soft toy, stock small recording and playback gadgets that can be used to record a teddy bear's growl. These have an inbuilt button that when pressed – or when the teddy's stomach is squeezed

ABOVE You can play full piano pieces from the music room, or scales to suggest practising.
Maker: Emma Waddell

BELOW The sound of a bell could suggest that the master of the house is calling a servant.
Maker: Ann Taylor

Two become one

A long-standing love of lighthouses lead Brae Oktober to create Walnut Bay Light, a beacon in miniature.

IN CREATING WALNUT BAY LIGHT, American miniatures and lighthouse enthusiast Brae Oktober has combined not just two passions, but two dolls' house kits. She first had the idea to build a lighthouse when Hobby Builders Supply used its Charming Cottage kit as the basis for one of its annual Creatin' Contests. She had initially planned to build a lantern room on top of the single-storey cottage, but having done some research and looked back at old photographs of lighthouses, she decided that this would not produce quite the impression she was after. But combining it with a Greenleaf Dollhouses' lighthouse kit would.

'I decided to split the cottage in half and emulate a structure like the Chicago Harbor Light,' she said. Situated at the south end of one of the breakwaters protecting the harbour in Illinois, USA this real-life lighthouse has a round tower, rather than an octagonal one. But in many other respects, Walnut Bay Light is very similar.

Customizing the kits was no simple task. The two kits were made of different materials. One was ⅜in (9.5mm) thick MDF and the other was ⅛in (3mm) thick plywood. 'Merging the two required some new walls to be cut... and a lot of patience!' Coating the two kits with a mixture of stucco and latex house paint brings harmony to the exterior and disguises the separate origins of the tower and cottage.

Brae also reduced the height of the tower to get the proportions she wanted, but this left no room for the middle floor. Instead, she added a spiral staircase not present in the original kit that runs the full height of the tower to reach the light (see page 120). This was made from scratch using plastic sheeting, the metal stake that came with an orchid plant, some wooden spindles, wooden beads, jewellery findings and brass wire.

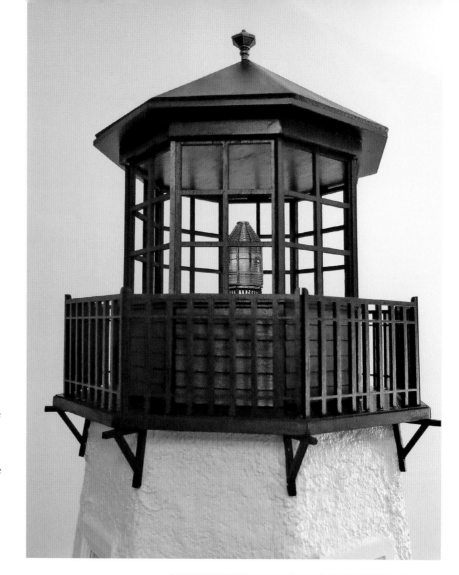

ABOVE The light is made from a converted Christmas decoration.

RIGHT The bedroom is a cosy retreat from the elements.

RIGHT The bin is a converted coffee creamer container.

Other elements of the house display similar creativity and ingenuity. The Fresnel lens in the lantern room was a Christmas ornament made by Harbour Lights, which she lit from underneath with a Car-Kit Beacon Light. Wall lights are encased in dolls' hair rollers to make them look more industrial, coffee creamer containers have been transformed into rubbish bins and foam curlers were cut in half and attached to the concrete pier to form fenders.

The pier particularly hides its origins well. It started as a wooden box, which Brae coated with a speckling compound and gel to create texture and hide the wood grain. Then she painted this grey, and added layers of brown, green and blue paint to achieve the look of weather-beaten concrete. The stippled green along the bottom suggests algae growth and really adds the final realistic touch.

ABOVE The landing is ideal for stargazing.

LEFT The base has been weathered to give the impression it has been battered by the tide.

BELOW The bathroom is small but contains all the essentials.

ABOVE As in a real-life lighthouse, Brae Oktober has had to squeeze rooms into the tiniest of spaces. The kitchen is well equipped for making tea, however.

BELOW The spiral staircase leads to the light.

Lighting and wiring

The warm glow of a fire or a lamp shining out from a corner is a sure-fire way to make any miniature scene appear instantly more realistic. Wiring a dolls' house is seen by many miniaturists as a daunting prospect, though it does not need to be.

GET YOUR IDEAS DOWN ON PAPER

The key to successfully wiring your miniature project is to plan it carefully and as early in the build as possible – certainly before you begin to decorate so that you can hide any wires from view. You may decide later that you have been too ambitious and need to scale back, but better that than finding out that you have insufficient capacity for the lights you have chosen.

For each room, you need to decide whether you want to fit ceiling lights, wall lights, lamps, or a combination of all three. Think about the placement of the lights and jot this down on a floorplan. This will help you to plan where you need to run the wires and how to conceal them. If you have a front-opening house, think about putting any wall lights on the back wall, rather than on the side ones. That means you will only need to drill a small hole in the back wall for the wires which will be covered by the light when you mount it on the wall. Ceiling lights are typically threaded through a hole in the ceiling and then run in a groove across the floor of the room above back to the main power supply.

It is worth giving special thought to how you are going to tackle attic rooms. Lights on chains work well, because they will hang correctly regardless of the slope of the roof.

Take time to consider the size of the lights too. Will a single pendant light be sufficient, or would you like a multi-branch chandelier? This is important when you come to select a power supply as you need one that is rated for the number of bulbs in your house. If you are not sure, or want to give yourself the flexibility to buy the dream light when you see it, err on the side of caution and list it as the biggest light

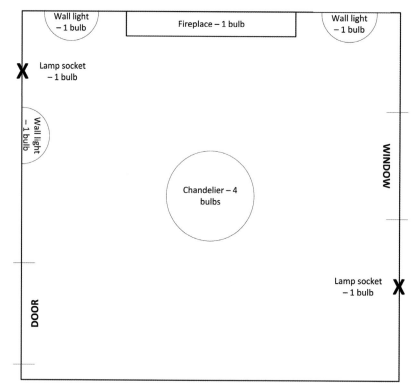

FRONT OF HOUSE

ABOVE AND BELOW When planning your wiring it is important to allow for all bulbs on each chandelier.

that you think you may use. There is no harm in designing your lighting system for a greater number of bulbs than you ultimately use, but putting in more bulbs than you had originally intended may risk overloading the system.

WIRING APPROACHES

Though it is increasingly possible to buy LED battery-operated lights, most lights you buy will require wiring. There are three possible approaches depending on how confident you are feeling and how much scope you want for future development.

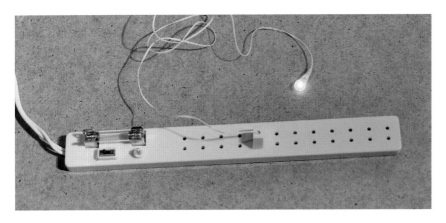

SOCKET STRIPS

The socket-strip method – sometimes known as twin wire – is the dolls' house equivalent of using a multi-way extension lead. You buy a socket board with a defined number of slots, an in-built fuse and its own dedicated power supply. Lights come with a length of twin-core wire and often a two-pin plug on the end. You need to run the wire from the light to a central point underneath or at the back of the house where you have decided to place the socket board and power supply. The lights simply plug in.

Standard plugs are typically about $^{25}\!/_{64}$in (10mm) wide. Unless you want to drill holes in each room large enough for the plug to pass through, you will need to remove the plug before you feed the wire round the house to the socket board. This requires you to pull out the brass plug pins, disconnect the wire and then reconnect it once you have passed the wire through the hole. It does not matter which wire is connected to which pin; the important thing is to ensure the wires do not touch.

The main limitation of using a socket strip is the number of bulbs and light fittings you can have. Standard strips only allow you to plug in 12 lights at a time. It is possible to get extension blocks but, in doing this, take care not to end up with too many bulbs for the power supply.

With most socket strips all lights come on together. It is possible to buy a connector strip with individual switches, but if you have mounted the socket board on the back of your house, it may not be particularly easy to get to the switches and turn them on and off.

BELOW Copper tape is a self-adhesive strip that you run to all points where power is needed.
Maker: Greenleaf Dollshouses/Darrell Payne

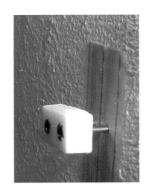

COPPER TAPE

Copper tape is a self-adhesive strip with two parallel layers of embedded copper to conduct electricity. The tape is run to all the points where power is needed and lights joined to the circuit either by soldering, or by inserting a pair of eyelets into the tape to form a socket. You will also need to connect the circuit to a power supply.

This approach requires considerable skill and is not generally recommended for the beginner. The copper in the tape is unprotected, which means it is at risk of corroding, particularly if it comes into contact with glue or water. As a result, it is often best – particularly for front-opening houses – to feed the twin-core wire from the light to a strip of copper tape running up the back of the house, rather than try to conceal the tape under wallpaper or flooring.

BELOW The lights need to be soldered to the tape, or can be plugged into a socket inserted into the tape.
Maker: Greenleaf Dollshouses

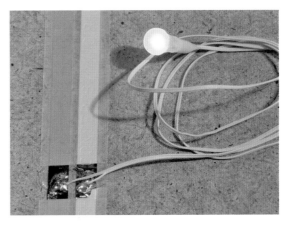

As with the socket-strip method, if you only use copper tape at the back of the house, you will need to remove the plug from the light fitting to be able to feed the wire through to the rear before joining it to the circuit. Using copper tape eliminates the need to have dozens of wires trailing down the back of the house, as with the socket-strip method.

It is possible to create separate circuits, for example for each floor, by installing discrete runs of tape. These can be joined by solder or by brass pins to build a bigger circuit, or you can have separate power supplies for each if you are worried about there being too many bulbs on one circuit. All lights on the same circuit will be on at the same time.

DISCRETE WIRES

Running discrete wires to the individual light fittings in each room offers a greater degree of flexibility if you are keen to operate rooms independently. It also gives you scope for expansion as your confidence grows, allowing you to add flicker units (see pages 106–107), sound (see pages 124–125) and remote control later (see pages 82–83).

Multi-core cable such as the type designed for burglar alarms is ideal. Individual cables can be run from the power supply to each room or floor of the house and then two cores split off from the central cable to each point where power is needed. It is essential to keep good records of which core goes where, so that you know which one powers the ceiling light in the lounge as opposed to the fire.

Many people are nervous of this approach because they feel it will require a lot of soldering. However, this can be easily avoided by using crimp connectors which allow two cores to be joined simply by inserting them into the connector and then compressing to force the wires together. As such, the multi-core approach requires less technical skill in some ways than using copper tape.

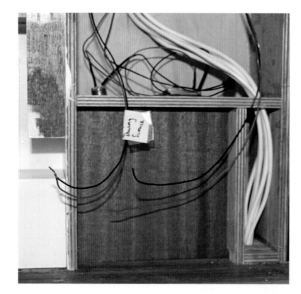

LEFT, BELOW AND BOTTOM Wires need to be recessed into the floor, or can be concealed within chimney breasts. In all cases, it is important to label which wires do what.

POWER SUPPLIES

Miniature lighting systems operate on a safe low voltage, usually 12 volts, compared with a UK mains supply of 240 volts, or 110 volts in the US. The higher voltage mains supply is converted to 12 volts and from an alternating current (AC) to a direct one (DC) within the power supply by an electronic circuit.

Historically, a transformer was used for this and you may still see a power supply referred to as such. Modern power supplies use a more efficient design of electronic circuit, which is smaller and lighter in weight meaning it can be housed within the plug.

In choosing a power supply, it is important to pay attention to the rating, expressed in amps (A) or milliamps (mA). The rating determines the number of bulbs that the unit can safely power. The grain-of-wheat or screw-in candle bulbs that are typically fitted in miniature lights take 30-50mA (or 0.03-0.05A) each, so a 1A power supply will be safe to power 20 bulbs.

There is no problem in using a 1A power supply to operate fewer than 20 bulbs, but you would not want to exceed this number. Equally, you do not need a power supply with a significantly higher rating, e.g. a 5A supply, if you only have 10 bulbs; the fuse within the power supply may fail to blow if there is a problem with the wiring. The table below provides an indication of the number of bulbs you can operate using a power supply of a given rating.

ABOVE The adaptor above clearly shows both the CE mark and the square within a square logo.

BELOW Suitable connectors could be used to join the power supply to the dolls' house wiring.

It is essential to check the label on the power supply for:
- The European CE or US FCC mark which shows that the power supply has been certified as safe
- A symbol of a small square within a larger one, indicating that the power supply is double insulated
- The listed input and output. The input denotes the voltage going into the power supply; an approved input of 240V AC is safe to plug into European mains power (110V in the US). The output shows the output voltage and rating in amps or milliamps; here you would be looking for an output of 12V DC and a rating of 1A (1000mA) to be confident that the device is suitable for powering your 20 bulbs.

If you are unable to find a label on the power supply that clearly lists its input and output or the appropriate safety symbols, then do not be tempted to use it. Avoid using a laptop power supply as that is unsuitable. Equally, do not use a power supply that shows signs of damage.

Having chosen your power supply, you will need to connect it to your wiring. If you are using a socket strip kit, the power supply should come ready to plug into the strip. If you are using copper tape or multi-core wiring, you may need to join the two together with a suitable connector or by soldering.

Rating	Number of bulbs
0.3A (300mA)	6
0.5A (500mA)	10
1.0A (1000mA)	20
1.5A (1500mA)	30
2.0A (2000mA)	40
3.0A (3000mA)	60
4.0A (4000mA)	80

RIGHT The power supply circuit is in the plug that goes into your home's electrical supply.

RETAIL THERAPY

A SHOP OR CAFÉ IS THE PERFECT project for a miniaturist who develops a passion or an aptitude for making specific items. Several makers start by trying to model a cake or a loaf of bread in polymer clay and find that by the time they feel they have perfected the technique, they have enough confections to feed a miniature army. Their only option for realistically displaying their handicraft is to open a miniature store.

For Sara Read, it was the sheer diversity of her miniature collection that drove her to create a shop. Only in an antique store would you find such a wide range of china, ornaments and curios.

Depending on the style of property, it is possible to have a retail outlet on the ground floor with living space above, or to go the whole hog and create a department store, with multiple different retail settings in the one building.

Many miniaturists favour the former option. A dolls' house that has sufficient rooms to accommodate a convincing department store will take up a lot of display room. Combining a shop with a flat or maisonette above also creates two different settings, providing options for displaying a miniature collection where it looks best. Emma Waddell has successfully done both, however.

OPPOSITE Though barely more than a few inches deep, this shop window is crammed full of treats to tempt children inside.
Maker: Gale Bantock

To look realistic, shops need to be full of wares, with multiples of the same item displayed alongside each other or stacked one on top of another. While in a designer boutique, you may have the occasional solo item – a one-off hat or handbag – in most cases you will want groups of at least three of each item. In grocery stores, you may need even more; a shop with only one or two examples of every item would look poorly stocked, but a display of just a couple of packs of biscuits alongside a wealth of other groceries would suggest that the shopkeeper is simply running low on the most popular lines and needs to reorder stock.

Careful thought needs to be put into where you place the various piles. In a real general store, large items would be too big and heavy to go on a shelf and would typically be left on the floor. However, it is quite easy to get carried away and take up a lot of floor space with various displays, such that miniature shoppers would be unable to get to the counter to make a purchase.

If you are short on space, or just dipping your toe into making shop scenes, a shop window is a good place to start and a diorama easily fits on a shelf. Giving it a seasonal theme, as Jean Nisbett has done, means that the display could also double as a Christmas decoration.

SHOP WINDOWS

BELOW Featuring a chemist, a boutique, a butchers, a fishmongers and a grocery and hardware store, this parade of shops features everything the miniature shopper needs. There is even a pub and a French-style pâtisserie where people can relax after all that shopping. *Maker: Emma Waddell*

ABOVE A love of all things English inspired this beautiful book and antique shop. It took a year to make, but Gerry de Cave admits most of that was spent staring at the room box and working out engineering challenges like where to put the wires so that they were concealed, but still accessible when it is time to change the bulb.
Maker: Gerry de Cave

BELOW A prolific creator of miniature food, Joelle Dade sells many of her creations. However, she needs somewhere to display the ones she keeps for herself. This French street with its boulangerie and delicatessen makes the ideal home.
Maker: Joelle Dade

ABOVE A shop window makes the perfect display for a small collection of themed miniatures. This window display serves as a unique Christmas decoration.
Maker: Jean Nisbett

Flowers and flint

Inspired by the flint houses of Norfolk, UK,
Liz Davis created an ideal base for a garden
designer to work and live.

VINTAGE HARDWARE AND GARDENING
store, Rosmarinus, is modelled on the brick and flint
buildings commonly seen in East Anglia, UK. It is
located in a small town not far from the North Sea
coast, attracting locals and the odd tourist keen to
have a rummage around the shop. Liz Davis had long

ABOVE The cabin features
an eco-friendly log wall.

LEFT Rosmarinus is a
garden hardware store
and landscape gardening
business.

BELOW Bricks were used
to create patterns
reminiscent of traditional
brick and flint buildings.

ABOVE The cabin provides a studio for the landscape gardener to meet clients and work on new designs.

LEFT The cabin features an environmentally friendly planted roof.

ABOVE The shop features an enticing array of gardening supplies.

BELOW Weeds in the gravel give the impression that the cabin has been there for some time.

had a love of houses of this style but once she decided to make one she found that East Anglian brick and flint buildings are rarely modelled. This meant that she would have to work out how to replicate the design through trial and error. She was keen to get it right, 'because most of the time, it's the outside of a mini building that we see'.

Liz started by edging each face with brick slips from Richard Stacey and then added horizontal lines and diamonds in brick to create the detail of the design. The remainder of each façade was then covered in mortar, so that the flints could be stuck on at random. Windows were cut in the roof and then the roof tiled with real slate.

'I wanted to use as much natural material as possible, even down to the gravel-covered base board that everything sits on,' she explained.

Next door she added a studio where a garden designer can work. She bought the frontage with its sliding door online, but the remainder of the building was constructed from scratch. To ensure it had the best green credentials, the studio features a roof covered in grass and plants. These were created from a mixture of railway scenic modelling materials and plants that she made herself.

The studio also has a log wall on one side, something that Liz would love to have in a property in real life. The gate made of old tools is another feature that she would love to replicate in full size.

But it is aspects such as the snail on top of the studio roof (from Tiny Tail Miniatures), the lichen on the flower pots and the dandelion weeds at the base of the log wall that are the perfect finishing touches, lending the project both realism and charm.

Making clothes

By making a few items of clothing, you can easily fill those empty pegs in your hallway, hooks on the back of the door or wardrobes.

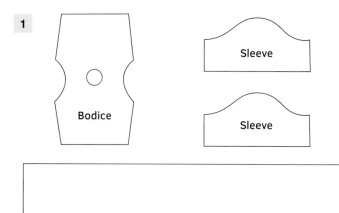

DRESS

1 Cut out a bodice 2⁷⁄₁₆ x 1³⁷⁄₆₄in (62 x 40mm), two sleeves 1 x 2in (25 x 50mm) and a skirt 6⁷⁄₆₄ x 22⁴¹⁄₆₄in (155 x 575mm) in your fabric.

2 Fold the bodice in half with the right sides of the fabric together and stitch the side seams. Press the seams open. Turn up a small hem around the bottom of the bodice and turn the bodice the right side out. Turn up a small hem along the bottom of each sleeve.

3 Fold the first sleeve in half and stitch the underarm seam. Press the seam open and turn the sleeve the right side out. Run a gathering thread around the top and bottom of the sleeve. Pull up the top gathering thread until the top of the sleeve fits over the armhole, while allowing the raw edge to turn under. Slip stitch the sleeve to the dress around the armhole. This can be easier if you slip a pencil or thin dowel through the bodice while stitching. Repeat for the other sleeve.

4 Turn up a small hem along the bottom of the skirt. Stitch the back seam and press the seam open. Run a gathering thread around the waist of the skirt. Gather up the waist of the skirt until it fits inside the bodice. Spread the gathers evenly around the skirt. Slip stitch the bodice to the skirt.

5 Pull up the gathering thread around the bottom of each sleeve to make a puff sleeve. Trim around the neckline and back opening. Use a small scrap of lace as a collar. Add small ribbon bows to the sleeves and neck and a piece of ribbon around the waist.

SHIRT AND TIE

1 Cut out two shirt bodies 2 x 3in (50 x 75mm), two sleeves 2⅛ x 2⅞in (54 x 73mm) and the collar 2 x ⅜in (50 x 9.5mm) in your chosen fabric. The collar should be cut from a double thickness of fabric, with both pieces glued together.

2 With right sides together, stitch the shoulder seams. Press the seams open. Cut a strip of fabric ²⁵⁄₆₄ x 2¾in (10 x 70mm). This will be for the mock front button band. Turn the raw edges inwards and glue the band down the centre front of the shirt. Turn up a hem at the bottom of the front and back. Stitch the side seams and press the seams open.

3 Turn up a small hem along the bottom of each sleeve on to the right side of the fabric. Then do it again to create mock cuffs. With the right side of the fabric facing, stitch the sleeve seam. Press the seam open and turn the sleeve right side out. Sew a gathering thread around the top of each sleeve and turn in the edges.

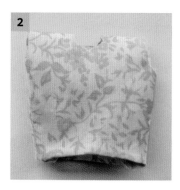

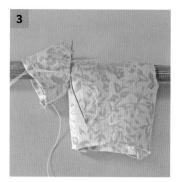

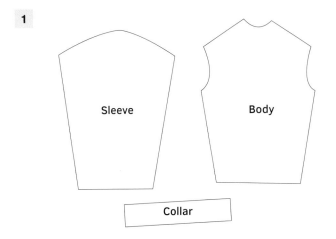

Sleeve

Body

Collar

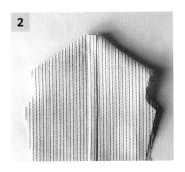

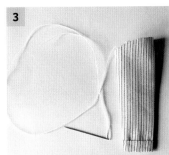

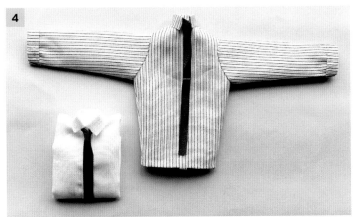

TROUSERS

1 Cut out two trouser pieces 2 x 3in (50 x 75mm) in your chosen fabric.

2 Turn up a small hem at both the ankle and waist. With right sides together, stitch the two pieces together along the centre front and back seams. Press the seams open.

3 Open up the trousers and align the legs. With the right sides still together, stitch the inner leg seam from the ankle hem to the crotch and then down the other leg. Clip the crotch, turn the trousers the right side out and press.

4 Add a waistband made from a thin strip of fabric. Turn the short raw edges in and fold the two long edges to the middle and glue in place.

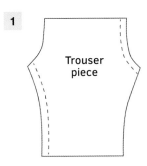

Trouser piece

4 Pull up the sleeve gathering thread until each sleeve fits on to the shirt and slip stitch or glue in place. Repeat for the other sleeve. Take the collar piece, press a tiny fold down from one long edge. Fold the collar around the neck and glue in place. Make a tie from silk ribbon and glue in place.

Add a tie pin by gluing on a row of no-hole beads.

TIP: To make clothing look worn, dampen it slightly, then paint the inside of the garment with a mixture of water and tacky glue. Crumple and leave to dry.

HIGH-STREET SHOPS

ABOVE Every conceivable kitchen aid and gadget is on display in this homeware store.
Maker: Amy Nikolai

ABOVE Former florist Diane Cooper has brought her work home with her, creating this miniature flower shop. It is built inside a converted rabbit hutch. She made the terracotta tiles from air-drying clay and filled the store with flowers found in haberdashery shops. Several of the display vases are recycled lipstick cases.
Maker: Diane Cooper

LEFT AND BELOW Having caught the bug for making miniature books, Sophie Anderson determined to keep going and create enough volumes to fill a bookshop. Like all good modern bookshops, it is also home to a café, so that you can grab a drink while you browse. The steampunk-style espresso machine was made from bullet casings.
Maker: Sophie Anderson

THIS PAGE Get all your shopping in one place. This department store offers everything from fish to furs.
Maker: Emma Waddell

Treasure trove

A miniature antiques store turned out to be the ideal way to house Sara Read's vast and eclectic range of miniatures.

YEARS OF COLLECTING MINIATURES that had caught her eye left Sara Read with a problem – one with which many miniaturists will be familiar. She had too many and they did not fit with the style of her main house. The way to display such a vast collection of items was to build an antique centre – and a sizeable antiques store at that, stretching over three floors.

Initially, Sara looked at buying a shop kit to house her collection, but quickly found that they were not big enough to accommodate all the items stored in boxes under the bed. So she decided to build her own, seeking inspiration for the right building on trips to Sussex – a UK county known for its antique centres.

Sara worked from photographs of a real building, though she modified it slightly. Thinking that a pitched roof may look too heavy, she changed it to

ABOVE The antiques shop was modelled on those in the UK county of Sussex. A third floor needed to be added to accommodate Sara Read's entire collection.

LEFT AND RIGHT Miniatures are piled on every available surface.

a flat one. The bay windows were also removed, as she was not sure she could replicate them faithfully, especially as she had chosen to glaze the windows with real glass. Wanting to keep the effect as realistic as possible, the roof was lined with real lead and the upper storeys faced in brick slips made from genuine brick.

However, even with all the effort to design an original home for her collection, she did not quite resolve the display problem at the first attempt. 'It took me a year to finish my original design, only to find it was still not big enough to house my complete collection, so I have spent the past year adding another floor,' admitted Sara.

But with the extra floor added, Sara could eventually begin to install the various miniatures. With such an eclectic array of miniatures, the display could easily have looked messy and disjointed. However, here Sara's keen eye for detail clearly shines through. Items are grouped on every surface, pieces of furniture placed one in front of the other and dolls and teddy bears piled into a cradle, just as they would be in an antique store in a small Sussex town.

ABOVE This shop sells everything – furniture, china, glassware and even a bear's head.

RIGHT AND BELOW Some of the delightful 'antiques' on sale in the shop.

Furniture

Whether creating a shop, pub or domestic house, you will need to build some furniture. Tables, chairs and shelves should provide you with the basics when you 'move in' to your miniature property.

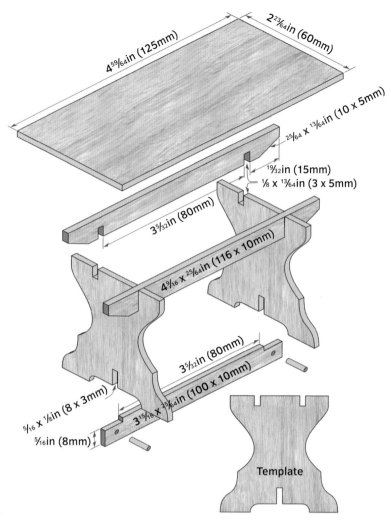

OAK TABLE

1 Sand both sides, along the grain, of a piece of ⅛in (3mm) thick oak sheet using medium and fine-grade sandpaper.

2 Draw, trace, scan or photocopy the two end templates. Temporarily paste on to the wood, allowing a ¾₄in (1mm) gap between them for the saw cuts. Mark out a piece 4⁵⁹⁄₆₄ x 2²³⁄₆₄in (125 x 60mm) for the top, two rails of 4⁹⁄₁₆ x ²⁵⁄₆₄in (116 x 10mm) and a third rail 3¹⁵⁄₁₆ x ²⁵⁄₆₄in (100 x 10mm), again allowing for the saw cut. By extending the length of the top and the three rails you can construct a longer table to suit your miniature room.

3 Drill ⅛in (3mm) holes at the ends of the six small slots on the leg template. Use a larger drill bit or a fret saw to cut the internal quarter curves of the feet. This will help you to cut out the wood in the internal corners and slots.

4 Cut all the parts using a fret saw fitted with a fine blade. A scroll saw, coping saw, or a bend saw with a suitable blade will also suffice.

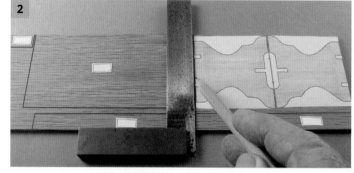

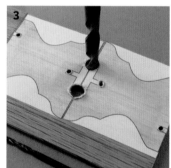

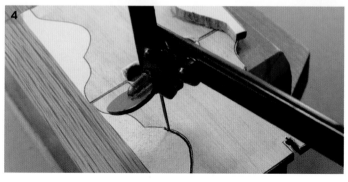

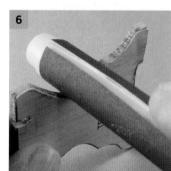

5 Use a mini drill to smooth and round the rough edges left by the saw. If you do not have a drill you can work the edges with a file and sandpaper wrapped around a dowel.

6 Give the ends a final smoothing with fine sandpaper stuck to the barrel of a marker pen (double-sided sticky tape works well for this).

7 File the small slots with a flat needle file (or a nail file). Keep testing the size of the gap using a scrap of the oak sheet until it slots in easily, but is still fairly firm.

8 Shape the bottom rail to fit. Drill a ⅛in (3mm) hole through each end. Cut the ends off a cocktail stick to represent the wedges. For a more authentic look, the ⅛in (3mm) holes can be filed square and a tiny oak wedge inserted.

9 Round the corner and edges of the table top on a sanding block. Paint, stain or polish each of the parts to achieve the finish you want, allowing at least an hour between coats.

10 Glue the framework together, then centre on the underside of the top. If you have polished the table parts, scrape off any wax before applying the glue.

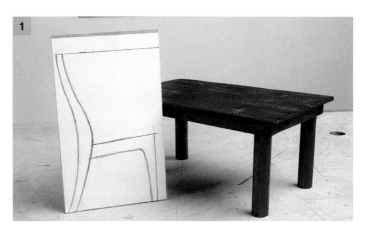

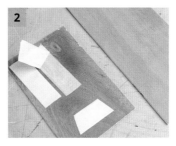

CHAIRS

1 Start by drawing a pattern of the chair on a piece of paper and spray mount the paper to a piece of plywood. This gives the shape and size required. The chair needs to be about 4²¹⁄₆₄in (110mm) high.

2 Stick the first piece of plywood (with the chair pattern on it) to a second piece with double-sided tape so they can be cut out together. The tape should be placed in areas that will not be cut, so that the assembly holds firm while you are working.

3 Use a coping saw with a fine tooth blade to cut around all the curves. Take care not to let the thinner sections break as you are cutting.

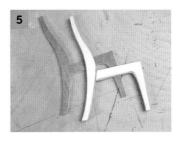

4 Use a wood file to clean up the shapes so the edges are even and properly matched.

5 You should now have two identical chair sides. Carefully remove the paper from the first one. The edges can be lightly sanded so there is no roughness.

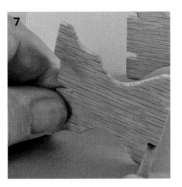
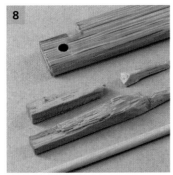

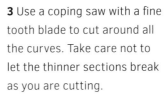

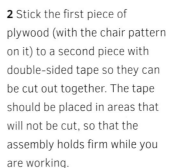

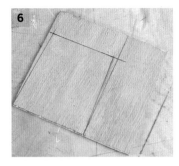

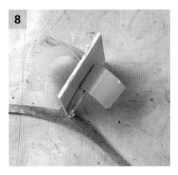

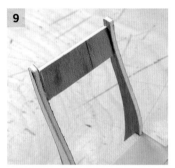

6 Mark a tapered seat on another piece of plywood. This needs to be the depth from the front edge of the sidepieces to the upright at the back.

7 Square off the edges with a block plane. Do not use sandpaper, which would round the edges and spoil the fit.

8 Glue and tape the seat and sides together. Make sure they are tightly held and the seat is flush with the top edge of the side pieces.

9 Cut a piece for the chair back. The ends should be slightly tapered using a sharp knife. It needs to fit nicely between the uprights of the chair sides. Sand the top and bottom edges and glue in position.

10 Add a back splat halfway up to give extra strength. It should be slightly bevelled in order to fit properly. Stain or paint your chair as required. Before doing so, it is important to clean away any excess glue.

RUSH SEAT

For a woven rush seat, you will need to cut a hole out of the seat base to make a frame. Then thread a needle with 3½–4in (90–100mm) of wet hemp cord. Glue the other end along the inside of the seat frame near the back. Take the needle over the back of the seat frame close to the side, then over the side at right

SHELVES

1 Cut the frame from strips of ⅛in (3mm) thick plywood. The sides of the shelves are made from strips $^{15}/_{16}$in (24mm) wide, the top from $1^{1}/_{16}$in (27mm) strips, the middle shelf from a $^{53}/_{64}$in (21mm) strip and the lowest shelf is a $^{43}/_{64}$in (17mm) strip. The shelves and the scalloped top rail are all 3⅝in (92mm) long and fit inside the side pieces, which are 3$^{15}/_{16}$in

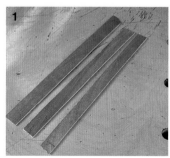

angles, again staying close to the back. Then do the same on the opposite side of the frame. Continue to go over and under the opposite rail and over and under its adjacent rail filling in the space in the middle. You should have four diagonal lines meeting in the centre. When you run out of cord, glue a short tail under the woven seat and begin a new piece.

(100mm) long. The top will slightly overhang the front and ends once the shelves are in position.

2 Carefully cut each piece to its finished length, using the fine tooth saw and a crosscut guide for accuracy.

3 Gently sand the edges with a block plane or rub on a sheet of medium-grade sandpaper.

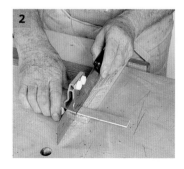

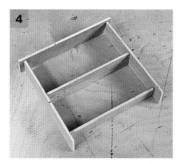

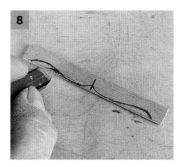

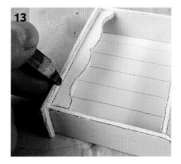

Keep each piece perpendicular as you work so that the edges are square.

4 You should have a dry construction that looks like this. Check it all looks correct before you go any further in case any of the components look out of shape and need remaking.

5 Draw the side profile on one of the side strips. Stick the two side pieces together with double-sided tape so they can be shaped together. Trim away most of the waste with a saw, then use a flat file to shape to the lines.

6 Sand the front edges to round them off.

7 Mark the position of the middle shelf, then glue all components together with PVA glue. Use an artist's brush to gently wipe away excess glue.

8 Draw and cut the scalloped top rail. Draw one half on a piece of paper or card and transfer that to the wood then flip it to get the mirror image.

9 Grip the top rail firmly in a vice and use a half-round file to create the shape. Keep checking as you go that both halves look identical.

10 Make the back panel. This can be compiled from strips of plywood $^{19}\!/_{32}$in (15mm) wide stuck to a backing card, or cut from a single piece. Drawing lines with a carpenter's pencil on the painted board at $^{19}\!/_{32}$in (15mm) spacings will give the same impression.

11 Glue the top rail in place. Once the glue is dry, paint the whole unit.

12 Apply PVA glue to the back edges with a small artist's brush, then carefully align the shelves over the backing piece. Place a weight gently on top until the glue has dried and then use a sharp knife to cut carefully around the outside. The shelves should simply pop out of the backing.

13 To give a suggestion of mouldings, use a flat carpenter's pencil to draw along all the edges. Just the lightest of lines will give quite a convincing effect.

TIP: Make two shelf units of different depths and mount the smaller one on top of the larger to make a basic dresser.

CAFÉS

ABOVE There is a tempting selection of cakes and pastries on offer for shoppers in the café of Emma Waddell's department store inspired by the television series *The Paradise*.
Maker: Emma Waddell

BELOW Irene McCulloch 'knocked through' the wall on the ground floor to make one large space to set out her classic Yorkshire tearoom.
Maker: Irene McCulloch

RIGHT It would be difficult to know what to choose from the vast array of cakes on the counter at this café.
Maker: Amy Gross

PUBS AND BARS

ABOVE AND RIGHT A visit to a restored saloon in Arizona, USA sparked the idea for this bar and bordello set in 19th-century San Francisco. Then careful planning and plenty of time spent watching repeats of classic westerns helped to refine the look.

Maker: Kathleen Stewart

BELOW The Ship public house is based on the 'spit and sawdust' pubs that Emma Waddell frequented on Friday afternoons when working in the City of London, UK. It was built largely to appease her husband, Stephen, who had been suggesting she make a pub for years.

Maker: Emma Waddell

BELOW Félix is regularly seen propping up the bar at La Luciole, a French bar from the turn-of-the-century Belle Époque era.

Maker: Jo Medvenics

Making food

Polymer clay is ideal for making miniature banquets. Available in a wide range of colours, it can be moulded to form bread, cakes, fruit and vegetables, as well as pies and roast dinners. Once you have mastered the basics of moulding and texturing the clay described here, you can make any foodstuff that you can think of.

ROAST CHICKEN

This project uses Fimo polymer clay in sahara.

1 Shape the clay into an egg shape measuring $^{25}/_{32}$ x $1^{3}/_{16}$in (20 x 30mm). Create a groove down the middle using a needle tool. Lightly dust the chicken with soft pastels in shades of brown to build up the 'roasted' colour on the outside. Fashion two wings and two thighs for the chicken. Colour them with pastels as before and position them in place on the body of the chicken.

2 Add texture to the chicken by pricking small clusters of holes into the body and thighs.

3 Gently cut through the breast with a sharp blade as if you were carving a slice of a real chicken. This will expose the Sahara clay inside. Cut two slices. Texture the exposed chicken breast and slices by scratching small lines into the surface of the clay.

4 Bake the chicken for the time recommended by the manufacturer. Once cooled, glue the chicken on to a plate or roasting tin. Glue a thin piece of white twine around the chicken's legs.

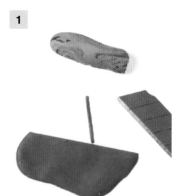

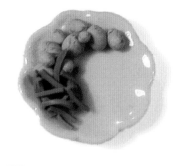

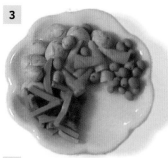

VEGETABLES

This project uses Fimo polymer clay in several colours: sahara, brown, dark green and translucent orange.

1 Marble the sahara clay with a little of the brown clay, then roll into oval balls of various sizes to create new potatoes. Roll out a piece of dark green clay to $^{3}/_{64}$–$^{5}/_{64}$in (1–2mm) thick. Using a bare blade, cut into strips $^{3}/_{64}$ x $^{13}/_{64}$in (1 x 5mm) to form green beans.

2 Use the translucent orange clay to create tiny carrots, creating small cones. Create a cluster of peas by rolling balls of dark green clay $^{3}/_{64}$–$^{5}/_{64}$in (1–2mm) across. Bake the finished pieces for the time recommended by the manufacturer.

3 Once baked and cooled, glue the vegetables on to the plate with a slice of chicken and some cutlery.

4 To add gravy, cover the vegetables as desired with translucent brown Deco Sauce. Leave the pieces to dry thoroughly.

BREAD

This project uses Fimo polymer clay in several colours: white, translucent white, ochre, gold yellow and champagne.

1 Mix the translucent white and white clay in a ratio of 3:1, adding tiny amounts of ochre, gold yellow and champagne and roll a loaf shape $^{25}\!/_{64}$ x $^{25}\!/_{32}$in (10 x 20mm).

2 Make a series of light indentations on the surface of the loaf shape using a rolled ball of tin foil and some sandpaper. Lightly dust with soft pastels, building up the colour gradually.

3 Take a craft knife and cut the 'crust' off one end of the loaf. Now using the larger end of a nail art dotting tool, lightly press all over the exposed white clay so that it recedes slightly from the outer 'crust'.

4 Next use a needle tool to make lots of tiny holes all over the white clay. Make sure that the holes are very close together, but not quite touching. Once you have done this, take the needle tool again and lightly create circle shapes over the surface so that you create tiny crumbs.

5 Cut a thin slice from the loaf with a craft blade, this will be your first slice of bread. It is much easier to add the detail first then cut the slice out as the sliced piece of bread can get easily distorted when worked on. Add detail to the newly exposed area of the loaf in the same way as before.

TIP: When working with polymer clay, try not to over handle it. If the clay goes too soft while you are working with it put it in the freezer for a few minutes to stop your piece from distorting. Use a glass or ceramic tile to work on as it helps your clay stick to the surface and stops it from moving around.

TIP: When creating miniature scenes and settings, think about adding little extras that will maintain a realistic feel such as a dab of gravy on a knife or fork.

ABOUT TOWN

JUST AS A MINIATURE SHOP ALLOWS the maker to concentrate on creating a particular item or group of items, so too can a miniature factory, workshop or museum.

Chocolates, canned goods, toys or food can be made to roll off the production line in a large property. A smaller model might lend itself to an artisan workshop. Any factory or workshop will be full of items in various states of production from barely started to fully packaged and ready for dispatch. There may even be the occasional abandoned or broken item.

Every modeller has a pile of early craft experiments that were progressing really well until the last minute when they were a little heavy-handed and snapped a delicate piece. This happens to craftsmen in real life as well as in miniature, so why not put the broken item on display? Or simply use the pieces that came out alright and dump the rest, suggesting an item in construction.

If you have a specialist themed collection, such as a range of oriental items from needlework to chinaware and statues, then maybe a museum could be the answer. Alternatively, where better to display a collection of miniature artworks than in a gallery? Miniature artists love copying the work of

OPPOSITE The Maritime Museum houses Robert Off's collection of nautical accessories and paintings. Built in a simple room box, the maker has added false walls to give the impression that the gallery continues beyond what you can see.
Maker: Robert Off

grand masters; you may not feel that your miniature family could afford to have a copy of a famous painting in their house, but it could certainly hang in a miniature museum.

Workshops and museums can be easier to arrange. Many craftsmen are disorganised, leaving piles of plans and half-finished items all over the house. The artist in Adam Fray and Lauren Hicks's house has daubed paint on every surface. Museums are a showcase, not a lived-in home. It is important that everything can be clearly seen and that there is enough space to circulate but exhibits can realistically be placed in the middle of the floor.

You can also add out-of-scale items. Museums are home to large sculptures that may have previously graced the exterior of a building, not just domestic items and artworks. A toymaker would be making smaller scale items; in a 1:12 scale workshop, this offers the chance to add a 1:144 scale dolls' house.

Non-domestic properties can still be challenging. You will certainly have to be more resourceful in your search for accessories and even make a lot of items yourself from scratch. However, for many miniaturists the need to make more than you buy will only add to the thrill of the project.

GALLERIES AND ARTISTS' STUDIOS

RIGHT An octagon is a tricky shape to use as a domestic setting due to the unconventional room layout. However, with a window on every side and lots of natural light, it is the perfect setting to house Peter Dryden's miniature paintings.
Maker: Peter Dryden

BELOW Rosie's Craft Cottage is the ideal space from which to run a small business making clothes and running craft courses. It has a cutting table, a desk at which the owner can sketch out her designs and a cosy corner where she can curl up with a magazine and seek inspiration.
Maker: Heather Macdonald

154

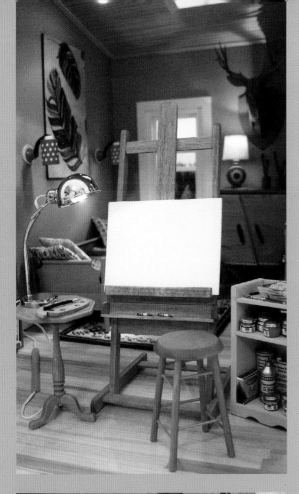

LEFT With 18 rooms over six floors, Maria Malmström's dolls' house is the miniature equivalent of a converted warehouse. Family apartments are cheek by jowl with artisan workshops. Here the carpenter has everything he needs to make toys, furniture and wooden ornaments. He even has a flask of tea for when he takes a break.
Maker: Maria Malmström

ABOVE AND ABOVE LEFT
A large window along one wall ensures that there is plenty of light by which to paint in this stylish artist's studio.
Maker: Brae Oktober

Paving and railings

With all the fixtures and fittings available for dolls' houses, it is always tempting to focus efforts on decorating the interior. But adding paving and railings can give a miniature property 'kerb appeal'. There is a wide range of different paving stones available from bricks to York stone slabs, but it is just as straightforward to make your own.

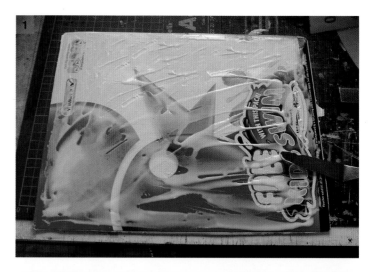

MAKING PAVING SLABS

1 Take a large sheet of card that is big enough to accommodate a standard-sized piece of sandpaper, or an equivalent-sized piece of textured wallpaper. Spread PVA glue over the surface of the card.

2 Apply the sandpaper or wallpaper to the glued area. Use a wallpaper roller to make sure that the paper is in even contact with the card. Weigh down the edges as there will be a tendency for the sheet to curl as the glue dries.

3 Paint the surface of the paper in a pale beige colour. Add a darker colour in random areas to give it the slightly weathered look of York stone and to produce slabs that vary slightly in tone. A combination of blues and greys will suggest slate or granite.

4 Once the last coat of paint is dry, coat the sheet with a matt varnish to seal it. Leave to dry, then cut the sheet into slabs 2²³⁄₆₄ x 1³⁷⁄₆₄in (60 x 40mm).

5 Apply a coat of paint to the baseboard to give the appearance of mortar between the slabs. When this is dry, glue the cardboard slabs into place leaving a tiny gap between each to let the mortar show through. Each row will need to be offset to give the effect of brick pattern paving.

TIP: Randomly gluing torn strips of paper on to the base surface to form layers is a good way to create a riven stone effect.

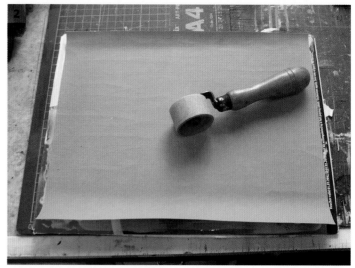

ADDING RAILINGS

These railings are made from brass brazing rods and pre-drilled brass strip, with beads added to create finials and rings for the detailing in the top rail.

1 Make a jig out of wood or MDF to hold everything in place while soldering. This just needs to be a simple grid made up of blocks as wide as the desired space between the railings separated by a gap the width of the brazing rod you are using. Remember to check the distance between the pre-drilled holes in the brass strip, as this will determine the spacing between railings.

2 Cut the brazing rods into approximate lengths, making everything slightly longer than you need for the final railings. They can be cut to size after soldering.

3 File the top of the rod to a point. This will form the final point on the finial. Then use fine sandpaper followed by methylated spirit to smooth and clean the pieces for soldering.

4 Lay the brazing rods in the jig with the points at the top and slide a length of pre-drilled brass strip over, followed by a second. The distance between the two brass strips should be the same as the gap between the brazing rods, thereby making a square, which will eventually hold a ring.

5 Solder the brazing rods to the brass strips. Use very thin solder and a hot soldering iron.

6 Drop a ring into each square and solder in place. The ring will drop to the bottom of the hole, meaning the wrong side is now uppermost.

7 Slide another pre-drilled strip on to the bottom of the railing and solder in place.

8 Remove from the jig and use an old toothbrush and methylated spirit to clean everything.

9 Glue three beads on to the top point to create the finial.

10 Cut the brazing rods to the right length at the bottom.

11 Spray paint everything with a coat of grey primer and leave to dry. Spray with black gloss paint. Several thin coats are best. A coat of scenic rust can be used to give the railings a weathered look.

RIGHT A jig made from MDF will help with the construction.

ABOVE Railings can be used to create a balcony, as well as a boundary to the house at street level.

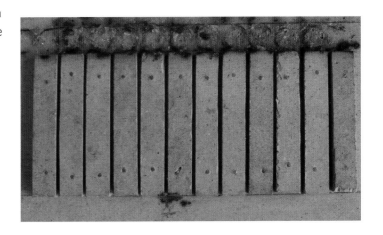

SCHOOLS AND CHURCHES

RIGHT Built in 1:24 scale, Little Acorns is the epitome of the village school, complete with two outdoor toilets.
Maker: Petite Properties

BELOW It is the arrangement of the dolls that give life to this little schoolyard scene. You can just imagine the two girls in the centre discussing the rules to some made-up game that only they understand.
Maker: Ingeborg Riesser

RIGHT A piece of scrapbooking paper picked up in an art shop was the starting point for this nursery school scene. The scene is brought together by reflecting colours from the paper in the various items and accessories. The yellow in the backdrop is repeated in the table and the sun wall motif.
Maker: Anna-Maria Sviatko

LEFT AND ABOVE The attention to detail in the chapel of Titania's palace is exquisite. The ceiling – based on images from the Book of Kells – took nine months to paint. The room also features an organ with working bellows, illuminated manuscripts on the lectern and the world's smallest rosary hanging on the prayer desk.
Maker: Sir Nevile Wilkinson

Stained glass

Stained glass is a prerequisite for any miniature church. However, this technique can be easily adapted for any building be it a grand house with its own private chapel, or a domestic house with coloured leaded lights or a glass panel in the front door.

1 First, you need to determine the size of your window opening. If you are working from scratch, this can be whatever size you would like; if you are customizing a kit, you will need to carefully measure the aperture excluding the width of the frame – approximately ³⁄₈in (9.5mm) depending on the size of wood strips you are using.

2 Look for images of stained glass that you can print on to transparency film. You may need to adjust the size of these images before you print them for a good fit. It is a good idea to print them on plain paper first to test the size. You can also crop the image to get the best fit. Create a cardboard template of the window and position it over the test image to decide on the best section to use.

3 Once you are happy with your image, print it on transparency film and cut it out. Leave a border all the way around the image. This should be the width of the window frame, so that the transparency is the full size of the aperture.

4 Cut window frame pieces from ⁵⁄₆₄ x ¹³⁄₆₄in (2 x 5mm) wood strips to surround the coloured portion of the transparency. You will need two sets – one each for the front and back of the window. Stain and glue in place.

5 Fit the window in the aperture.

TIP: To determine the ratio by which you need to enlarge or reduce the image, take the height of your window opening and divide this by the height of the printed image. For example, if the image is 4in (100mm) high and the window is 4¾in (120mm), then the image needs to be increased by 20 per cent in both height and width.

MOUNTING THE WINDOW IN A ROOM BOX

If you have a room box, you can glue the window directly on to the back wall and hide the edges with the window casing. The image should be the full size of the aperture.

1 Cut and glue stained lightweight card ½in (12.5mm) wide to surround the coloured portion of the transparency. This will set the window back slightly.

2 Glue lightweight white card to the reverse of the image. This will be on the outside, so will not be visible, but will help to make the image more visible.

3 Cut strips of stained lightweight card to cover the edges of the window opening and the card setback. Temporarily fix the window to the outside of your room box to measure how wide the strips need to be. Glue the strips in place.

4 Glue the window in place.

5 Cut ½in (12.5mm) wide pieces of stained card to make window casings and fix them in place.

TIP: The same mounting technique could be used to add an exterior scene to the outside of a room box window, suggesting the street or garden beyond. However, print the image on solid card rather than transparent film.

UNUSUAL BUILDINGS

JUST AS IN REAL LIFE WHERE NOT everyone lives in a two-up, two-down house, miniaturists are increasingly moving away from just modelling traditional houses. The desire to take an old mill or warehouse and convert it into a chic loft apartment is just as strong in miniature as in the real world. Meanwhile, miniaturists with a strong sense of wanderlust are focusing their desire for travel into model caravans and mobile homes.

Miniature scenes do not have to be based around a distinct style of property either. Almost any container can be used to display miniatures. As with Julie Campbell's representation of Marie Antoinette in a bird cage, these dioramas can be quite symbolic. An unusual container such as a presentation box for a bottle of wine or a decorative brief case might simply be the perfect size to display a discrete selection of miniatures. It is quite common for miniaturists to fall in love with an item that they find at a dolls' house fair which is entirely out of keeping with the age and style of the main property that they are modelling. Instead of having to walk reluctantly away empty handed, it can form the basis of a separate diorama.

Equally, it may be a good way to redeploy an item that is sitting around unused. That gift of a terrarium may be well intentioned, but if gardening is not your

OPPOSITE This caravan started life as a quirky wooden bird box before being transformed into a delicious pink cupcake stall. Swapping the wooden wheels on the bird box for model airplane wheels and covering the outside with corrugated cardboard helped to give that vintage trailer look.
Maker: Kim Saulter

thing, then the terrarium could end up sitting in a corner gathering dust for years. As with any project, these unusual containers have their advantages or disadvantages. A terrarium or bird cage can be viewed from any angle, so it is important to build a scene that looks good whichever way you look at it. It may also be necessary to install a false wall that creates a background to the display and directs the viewing angle. A wine box is very tall and thin, so you will have to create a very focused display, or add shelves which allow you to put items on different levels.

However, there is no need to restrict yourself to a particular period. In contrast to a Victorian or Art Deco house, the exterior does not immediately suggest the style of the interior. This frees the miniaturist up to select the items they like; they do not have to have ones that would all logically sit together in a real house.

Meanwhile, as is the case for full-sized caravans, space in miniature mobile homes is at a premium. Careful planning is needed if you are to be able to incorporate all the elements you want. You many need to customize furniture to ensure it will fit in a tight or awkwardly shaped space.

CARAVANS AND MILLS

LEFT AND BELOW LEFT
Kim Saulter pored over pictures of real-life glamping sites to find inspiration for her retro caravan. A bike rack on the back is a must for any camper who wants to take off and explore the area around the campsite. Adding the rack also meant the model would actually sit level and genuinely look like it could be towed behind a car.
Maker: Kim Saulter

RIGHT Following a course on how to use white clay to make bricks, Jan Simpson Gilham set about turning the Rik Pierce witch's cottage kit into an old water mill. Pierce advised her to 'always give people plenty to look at'. She took him at his word. The yellow rose over the door has nearly 100 blooms!
Maker: Jan Simpson Gilham

LEFT AND RIGHT Built entirely from scratch using cardboard boxes covered in papier-mâché, Mill End is a classic village flour mill. Inside, Pam Veiler has used oddments of chain and pieces from broken small domestic appliances to create the grain hoppers and winches needed to haul bags to the top of the building for grinding.
Maker: Pam Veiler

Applying gold leaf

Gold leaf gilding is a method of applying a thin layer of real gold to any object. Most objects made from wood, metal, resin or plastic can be gilded. Using gold leaf will give a far better lustre than any brushed or sprayed gold paint. It can easily be used to cover the whole of a surface or just to pick out highlights.

GILDING A FRAME

1 Paint the picture frame with a coat of bright acrylic paint. This seals the frame, but will also help you to see what you have covered as you are working. If the material is very porous like plaster, it may need sealing with an extra coat of paint. Check and sand any irregularities as they will show through the gold leaf.

2 When thoroughly dry, brush on a thin coat of adhesive size. After 15 minutes the surface should be 'tacky' (about as sticky as a piece of tape) and ready to apply the gold leaf. There is no hurry as the sized surface should remain tacky and workable for several hours.

3 Keeping the gold leaf sandwiched between the tissue paper, cut the leaf into small sections of about $^{25}/_{64}$in (10mm) square. Leave a good gap between each piece you cut, as they have a tendency to be attracted to each other!

4 Rub a soft brush on your hair or skin to pick up a little oil; it will now pick up a piece of the gold leaf from the tissue. Alternatively, use the tiniest smear of petroleum jelly on the back of your hand and touch with the brush. Gently lay the gold onto the object, overlapping the joins by $^{3}/_{64}$–$^{5}/_{64}$in (1–2mm). Do not worry about crumpled areas, folds or gaps, as the gold is so thin it will blend together.

5 Continue until the object is completely covered and the gold is brushed well into the corners and mouldings. Any surplus gold will just brush away. These 'sowings' or small oddments can be useful for covering gaps or picking out highlights on other objects.

TIP: When working with gold leaf, always work in a draught-free area. If the leaf folds or crumples it can be flattened by gently breathing on it. Do not try to pick up the gold with your fingers because it will stick to your skin.

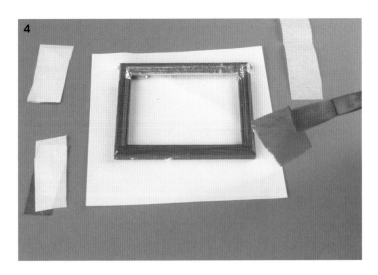

RIGHT Based on Burton Agnes Hall in Yorkshire, UK, this model shows a late Elizabethan house and garden occupied by a Stuart family in around 1640. The hall shows the dark heavily carved oak panelling, strapwork and semi-classical columns common in that period and is hung with many portraits in gilded frames.
Maker: John Hodgson/Hever Castle

UNUSUAL DISPLAY BOXES

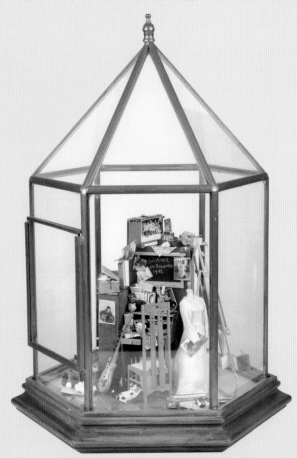

LEFT Christiane Berridge describes her scene in a terrarium as a '3D scrapbook'. It has been built in the round, so it can be viewed from any angle and when on display can be turned to reveal a new aspect to the miniature scene.
Maker: Christiane Berridge

RIGHT This piece is filled with symbolism. The gilded bird cage depicts French queen Marie Antoinette, who spent her final days imprisoned in La Conciergerie. The silk curtains conceal her view of the world, keeping her out of touch with the public. Instead she indulges her vanity with shoes and pretty trinkets.
Maker: Julie Campbell

BELOW A series of shelving units glued together makes a striking display. Stacking the shelves to achieve the desired messy effect is time consuming, but effective.
Maker: Jennifer Osmond Hatt

RIGHT A mini suitcase picked up in a 'designer labels for less' store is the basis for this miniature boutique to display the silk dresses, parasols and accessories that Eileen Lang has made and collected over the years.
Maker: Eileen Lang

BELOW Specializing in making 1:144 scale buildings, Nell Corkin is able to turn even the smallest container into a miniature scene. This has led her to creating a series of 'nut houses'.
Maker: Nell Corkin

Needlepoint carpets

Carpets, fire screens, samplers and many other household soft furnishings are made of needlework. The techniques are the same as full-sized tapestry or cross-stitch work. However, the base fabric is much finer and usually made of silk gauze.

STITCHING THE BASIC DESIGN

1 Mount the silk gauze in a stiff card frame to keep it taut while stitching. Use narrow strips of masking tape to attach the fabric to the card frame.

2 Sort the stranded cotton threads into colours, using the colour key to check that you have the right number of colours and to marry up the thread to the symbol on the chart. Read the instructions to identify how many strands of thread should be used; kits may vary anywhere between one and three strands at a time.

3 Start stitching the design in the centre of the fabric. This will ensure you will have an even border of 'waste' fabric all round and do not end up stitching too close to the edge. Remember that one square on the chart equals one stitch. Stitch the detail first and when all the detail is complete, fill in the background.

4 When the stitching is complete, press it face down over a soft pad such as a towel using an iron on a medium setting, pulling the fabric gently if necessary to make sure it is dead square.

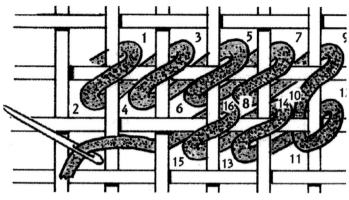

Tent stitch

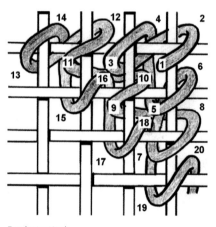

Basket stitch

BASIC TECHNIQUE

Kits are typically worked in tent stitch (similar to half cross stitch) for the detail and basket stitch for the background. When stitching always use a 'stabbing' motion and not a 'sewing' one. Begin each length by knotting one end and taking the needle from the front to the back of the silk gauze about ½in (12.5mm) away from where you intend to start stitching. Stitch towards the knot, securing the underlying thread as you go. Snip the knot off when you reach it. Finish each length by running the needle under a few threads on the back. This will keep the back tidy and ensure that lumps do not show through to the work at the front.

TIP: There are many miniature needlepoint kits available. When starting out, pay careful attention to the fabric count or holes per inch (hpi). This can be anything between 20 and 56. The higher the number, the finer the fabric and the more difficult it is to see the holes and the stitches you make.

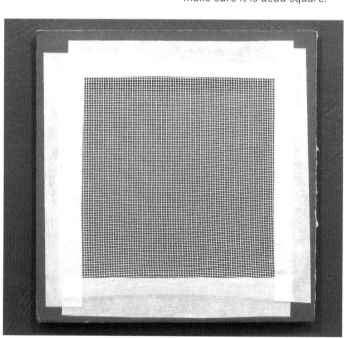

HEMMING A CARPET

Hemming is done using a double thickness of thread in the same shade as the final row of stitches. Thread the needle with one length about 30in (750mm) long, double it over and knot the ends together and run a few stitches through the back of the work near where you want to begin to secure it. Starting mid-way along a side is best.

1 Making sure the design is centred, trim the unworked gauze around the stitching to ½in (12.5mm) wide all round.

2 With the right side of the stitching facing you, turn the unworked canvas under (i.e. away from you) so that the first row of empty holes is along the edge of the carpet. Begin to oversew along the edge. Make sure that each stitch begins in the same hole as the outermost line of tent stitches and finishes two holes further away. The needle goes vertically through the two layers each time. This will give you the neatest edge. As you approach a corner (about ¾in (20mm) away), carefully fold down the adjoining edge and oversew around the corner

through the two thicknesses, working the very end stitches twice through the same hole to make sure that the bare canvas is properly covered. If, as you approach the corner, you have less than 8in (200mm) of wool left in the needle, finish off and start a new length now, as starting a new length just as you are stitching around the corner is tricky.

3 Once complete, take a length of stranded cotton in the same shade as the background of the carpet so that the stitches will blend as much as possible. Using a single strand, secure the thread and slip stitch the edge of the fabric lightly to the reverse of the needlepoint stitches, making sure that you do not pierce the front of your work while you do it. This will ensure that the underside remains flat and you have a smooth carpet like this one by Janet Granger.

TIP: After oversewing the edge, you may want to cut away some of the waste fabric at each corner to reduce bulk. Cut diagonally across each corner, but be careful not to cut too close to the stitching.

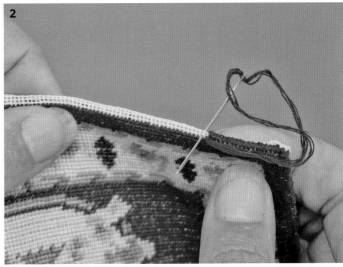

OUT OF THIS WORLD

THESE DAYS MINIATURISTS ARE increasingly turning to fantasy to escape the restrictions that they encounter when modelling real-life scenes as it allows them to combine items that come from different periods and would not normally be found together. Who is to say that in an alternative universe, people are not still cooking on coal-fired ranges, even though they have invented a time machine?

In this vein, miniaturists are increasingly tapping into the steampunk trend. A design style that combines historical elements with anachronistic technology, steampunk is an ideal place to start with modelling fantasy worlds. It takes Victorian items and embellishes them with cogs and wheels to invent all manner of gadgetry. Given the amount of Victorian accessories available to the dolls' house modeller, it is easy to source the base items. Then it is simply a case of letting your imagination run wild to decide how the item should be enhanced and adapted.

Josephine Parnell has taken another approach to combining fantasy with period accessories. Unable to find a style of doll she liked and that was suitable for dressing in costume, she defied convention and began making clothed teddy bears. The Edwardian bears

OPPOSITE After seeing a friend's post online about abandoned houses, Stan Gregg decided to create this haunted house. Having stood vacant for years, the roof is in need of repair. The inside is cluttered with the possessions of previous owners who appear to have left in a rush.
Maker: Stan Gregg

shown taking tea in this chapter are just a few of the many characters she has created, which range from Henry VIII bear and 'Elizabearth I' to contemporary bears in pyjamas.

For Karina Schaapman, modelling the vast higgledy-piggledy Mouse Mansion allowed her to create an imaginary world where the residents lived together in greater harmony without the prejudice she experienced as a child. The ramshackle miniature house has gone on to be the inspiration for a series of children's books about Julia and the other mice that live in the mansion.

But choosing to build a fantasy property could work the other way round. JK Rowling's Harry Potter novels have provided a rich seam of inspiration for dolls' house modellers. The extent of the world presented in the seven-novel series means that there is a magical version to be created of every style of house from the grand estate of Malfoy Manor to classrooms, shops and even the beach-front house to which Harry, Ron and Hermione escape in *Harry Potter and the Deathly Hallows*.

The only restraint in the fantasy miniature world is your imagination, so let your thoughts run wild and see what wonderful worlds you can create.

MAGIC AND MYSTERY

ABOVE AND RIGHT Combining Victorian style with elements of fantasy, this shop makes liberal use of cogs and gears – those essential elements of steampunk – above the doors and windows, as well as around the figurehead. A zip running down one wall reveals a brick exterior hiding beneath the stone façade.

Maker: Wildwood Dollhouses

ABOVE Boggart's Bazaar is the go-to place for bottles of pixie dust, unicorn horns, glowing pumpkins and other magical supplies.
Maker: Caroline McFarlane-Watts

LEFT With a background in shop merchandising, Jennifer Osmond Hatt naturally ended up creating miniature shop scenes. A love of antiquing paper and a style she describes as 'distressed vintage with a hint of chaos' has resulted in displays that would not look out of place in a Harry Potter film.
Maker: Jennifer Osmond Hatt

BELOW When the Pevensie children were called back to Narnia, hundreds of years after they had ruled as kings and queens, Cair Paravel was an overgrown ruin. It was only after they had been there several hours and had pulled the ivy from the door that they realized where they lit their fire had been the entry to the castle treasury.
Maker: Sue Cook

Ageing

Whether shop bought or made from kits, most miniature furniture and accessories arrive in a pristine condition. However, few houses – whatever their age – are totally devoid of cobwebs, piles of old newspapers, dirty plates, an unmade bed or the odd battered suitcase gathering dust in the attic. And some properties, including castles and wizards' lairs, simply do not look convincing without a layer of grime. To create that lived-in look, there are various things you can do.

A LAYER OF DUST

If you think about how you live in your own house, there are items that you have had for a while and other things that are new. You throw the latest issue of a magazine down on top of the ones that are already there, or toss your bag on the hall table that never moves. Dust settles on the things that have been there for a while undisturbed, while newer items will be a little bit cleaner. You want to reflect this in your house by creating layers with different amounts of dust on each.

Baby powder is ideal for creating a layer of dust. When the main items of furniture are *in situ*, such as bookshelves and sofas that are not likely to be moved very often, put a tiny amount of baby powder in the palm of your hand, hold it up to your face and blow

RIGHT Moss grows thickly on this tiled roof.
Maker: Karin Foster

BELOW A coating of baby powder will give the appearance of dusty floors.
Maker: Karin Foster

gently. This will distribute the powder across the room. You can then introduce the other items to the room; these will look like they have been moved more recently.

In rooms that are rarely used, such as the attic, you may want to make marks in the dust. 'Walking' across the room with dolls' shoes on your fingers will leave a trace of the last visitor. Or making marks using a cocktail stick could suggest that a mouse or other small creature has scurried across the floor at some point. Coating the floor afterwards with a fine mist of hairspray will set the marks in place.

Individual items can be given a layer of dust and grime by painting with a watered-down coat of acrylic paint (or wash) or dusting with a little chalk or eyeshadow. If you are modelling a scene that is based in a particular area, think about the colours of the exterior landscape and select chalks that reflect that. In the Australian outback everything gets coated in a reddish layer of dust; in Victorian London, the dusty air would have been thick with soot, giving everything a much blacker covering.

Green and grey washes and chalk or eyeshadow powder are useful when you want to suggest mildew or mould, for example, in a bathroom or laundry.

Cobwebs can be made using any fine fibres, such as wisps of quilt batting or soft toy stuffing, threads from laddered tights, sections of hairnet, or even strings of tacky or hot glue. These need to be applied sparingly and only in the corners of rooms where they would logically be.

AGEING SOFT FURNISHINGS

Curtains, bedspreads and old clothing are often faded through exposure to sunlight or slightly grey from frequent washing. There are a number of ways to tone the colour of the fabric down but, before applying any form of wash, it is worth considering whether you could use the fabric with the wrong side showing. This works particularly well for plain fabrics, as the wrong side is usually just a more muted version of the right side.

If this does not give you the look and feel you want, try painting the fabric with a thin wash of acrylic paint, dying it in some cold tea or coffee, or dusting with chalk or eyeshadow. You can also use a toothbrush to flick a wash of paint at the fabric; the dirty water used for washing your paint brushes is good for this.

Rubbing areas of the fabric with a bleach or laundry stain removal pen will create lighter spots. This is particularly effective for the leading edge of

curtains that may have been exposed to more intense sunlight. Remember that the inner part of a pleat, gather or fold would be darker than the outer part. Use a cotton bud to apply chalk to darken these areas.

A pounce bag is another useful device for ageing fabrics. Used extensively by television costume designers, pounce bags are small sachets made of loosely woven fabric. They are filled with cotton balls and a small amount of charcoal, baby powder, chalk dust or eyeshadow. You can then just tap the bag over the item, coating it with a small amount of dust.

UPHOLSTERED FURNITURE

Similar techniques can be used to distress armchairs and other upholstered furniture. The trick is to concentrate on the areas of the chair that would get the most wear such as the seat, the tops of the arms, the lower front of the chair where a person's legs would rub and on the back of the seat which would come in contact with the back of a person's head.

As with other fabrics, you can make the chair look dirty by coating it with watered-down brown acrylic paint, or by rubbing on a tiny bit of white paint with your fingers. This will not make the chair look white, instead it will appear slightly faded and grubby.

Sanding the fabric with a medium-to-coarse grade of sandpaper will roughen the surface and eventually cause the material to fray. For a really worn look, keep going until the wooden base of the chair is visible through the fabric.

A really worn chair may be ripped or torn. Making several small slits in the fabric very close together will replicate threadbare patches. Where the chair has worn through, make a single L-shaped tear with a craft knife. Place a wisp of toy stuffing in the hole, or maybe a rusty spring, to give the impression of the upholstery beginning to seep out.

A combination of these techniques will give your house the appearance of age, but do it sparingly and build up the effect in layers, as too much wear will look contrived and is difficult to reverse once done.

BELOW Sawdust has been scattered over the base to make it appear as if someone has recently been chopping up logs.
Maker: Karin Foster

ANIMAL BURROWS

LEFT Unable to find dolls suitable for dressing, Josephine Parnell turned to making bears as a way to indulge her passion for creating period costume. Here a group of well-to-do Edwardian bears take tea.
Maker: Josephine Parnell

BELOW Children and a variety of animals enjoy a rare opportunity to meet Father Christmas in this scene.
Maker: Dolph Gotelli

RIGHT These mice live in a rural setting. They have filled their hollow with things foraged from the fields around them. Straw provides insulation above the bed, fruits and nuts are stored in the basement for winter, while an empty nut makes a cosy cradle for baby mice.

RIGHT Like the Borrowers in the book by Mary Norton, Maggie Rudy's mice are resourceful, even turning a human fork into a rack for their pots and pans.
Maker: Maggie Rudy

The house that kept on growing

Mouse Mansion started as a single scene in an orange crate. But before long it had been extended and extended...

THE MOUSE MANSION IS A VAST higgledy-piggledy hive of homes, shops and a factory. Made entirely from scratch by Karina Schaapman, it started life as a single orange crate that seemed to be the perfect size to create a dolls' house and home for the mice that would feature in the children's book she had wanted to write for a long time.

The first crate was turned into a bedroom. 'I started with a patchwork quilt, added a little bed and a floor and a curtain. Then I added a bathroom and a kitchen,' Karina said.

After that, Karina felt that the mice would need somewhere to go to get their food and their clothing, as well as places to work, relax and play. So encouraged by her husband, she stuck more orange boxes together in slightly random configurations. The whole was then covered in papier-mâché to strengthen it.

The resulting warren has been filled entirely with things that Karina has made herself, from the plates on the tables to the lights and the flowerpots. This has allowed her to experiment with lots of different materials.

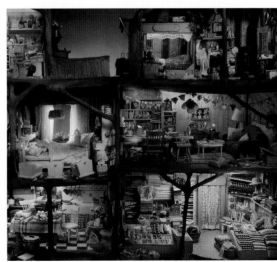

ABOVE AND RIGHT Mouse Mansion is a sprawling mass of rooms to which Karina Schaapman has continually added.

LEFT Julia lives with her mother at Mouse Mansion.

Life in Mouse Mansion is reminiscent of Karina's own life. For example, one of the two main characters in her book, Julia, lives alone with her mother. But the environment is a much more caring community without the prejudice and abuse that marred Karina's childhood. 'I wanted to build a world like the one you'd want for your kids, the one that so many grown-ups long for and many people have to do without.'

ABOVE AND RIGHT
Mouse Mansion houses everything the mice could need, including a hospital and a rag 'n' bone man.

LEFT Mouse Mansion even includes its own fully stocked leather goods shop.

Painting miniatures

Buying artisan-made pieces is a delight, but it can be hard on the pocket. For those lacking the skills to make miniatures from scratch, making them from brass and white metal kits or buying items that have been 3D printed or moulded in resin is a more cost-effective solution. When painting in miniature, any tiny mistake or blemish can be highly visible. Painting becomes easier with practice, but a few simple tricks will help even beginners get impressive results.

When working with a kit, the first thing is to decide whether it will be easier to paint the components and then build the kit, to paint the finished item, or to paint it at some stage mid-construction. At whatever point you are painting the item, you want to work on a smooth, clean and dry surface, so the first thing is to sand off any burrs left from the moulding or casting process and then wash and dry the item. Just use water, as some detergents contain lanolin and will prevent the paint from sticking.

ACHIEVING A GOOD RESULT

Metal and 3D-printed plastic models always require priming, so spray them with an acrylic primer. It is better to spray three or four thin coats, rather than one thick layer. A lot of modellers use a grey primer, but some prefer plain white because they feel that it creates a better base for bright colours; they are not 'muddied' by the grey underneath.

RIGHT Dry brushing with red paint has helped to give Punch and his friends a ruddy complexion.

BELOW A plain white metal bucket was converted into a period accessory by painting it and stencilling on the word 'fire'.

BOTTOM The right-hand car has a battered 'leather' roof.

You can then paint the items using enamel or acrylic paint. In most instances acrylic is best, but if you are painting an item that would be glossy or coated in enamel, such as kitchen scales or biscuit tins, then enamel can give you a more realistic finish.

The most important thing to get good paint results is to use good brushes – and for miniatures particularly fine brushes. Cheap brushes have a tendency to splay, making it hard to achieve the precision you want. They also have an annoying habit of 'moulting' and leaving bristles on your beautifully painted miniatures. Working in small scale, you will have to change your brushes regularly. Brushes that have begun to splay are, however, useful for dry brushing.

Start by painting the item as if it were new, working on the paler areas first. It is easier to cover white paint with black or navy blue than the other way around. You may need several coats of some pale colours to get a consistent coverage.

AGEING

Once the whole model is covered, you can begin to work on ageing and weathering to add depth and realism. Thin washes of paint or ink work well on etched metal kits, because the paint runs into the grooves, but leaves the higher areas the original colour. Dry brushing adds texture and age. You will need to load the brush with paint and then wipe most of it off on to a piece of kitchen paper. You can then brush over the item to add a hint of the new colour on top of the base coat. Repeating this process a few times with different shades can add depth and variation to a piece.

Once you are happy with the finished result, a fine coat of acrylic varnish will help to fix the item. A satin varnish can be used if you do not want too much of a sheen.

Tools and materials

You will need a wide selection of different items to create your miniature world. You will already have many of them at home while other more specialist tools and materials are readily available at craft shops and online.

GENERAL CRAFT TOOLS

Clothes pegs
A cheap and handy alternative to spring clamps for holding items together while glue dries.

Craft knife
Used for cutting wood and card. Always use with a cutting mat and steel ruler.

Cutting mat
A mat must be used when cutting with a craft knife to protect working surfaces.

Embossing tool
A hand-held tool with ball-shaped ends that create raised designs when used on polymer clay or metal embossing sheets.

Paintbrushes
Use artists' paintbrushes to apply paint and varnishes. They are available in a range of sizes.

Paper punches
Used to cut out shapes from paper and thin card. Available from craft shops in a variety of shapes and sizes, they are essential for making plants and flowers.

Ruler
An essential basic tool for accurate measuring and cutting. Always use a steel ruler when cutting with a craft knife.

Scissors
Essential for cutting all sorts of craft materials.

Toothbrushes
Useful for creating texture in render or items made of polymer clay, such as food and kitchen appliances.

WOODWORKING TOOLS

Block plane
A small plane that fits neatly in your hand that is useful for cleaning up the edges of pieces of wood.

Coping saw
A coping saw is a type of hand saw used to cut intricate external shapes and interior angles or cut-outs.

G cramps
G cramps come in various sizes. They are useful for clamping items to a bench. When using a G cramp, always insert a cramping block (small piece of wood or plastic) between the cramp and the item being clamped in place to distribute the pressure and to prevent damage. When cramping a joint take care not to squeeze out all of the glue.

Mitre block
A small metal or plastic block used to cut items at an angle. Slots in the block's side guide the saw.

Needle files
These have fine, shaped tips for intricate shaping and sanding.

Panel saw
A hand or panel saw is essential for cutting large pieces of wood.

BELOW Clamps and cramps are useful when working in small scale.

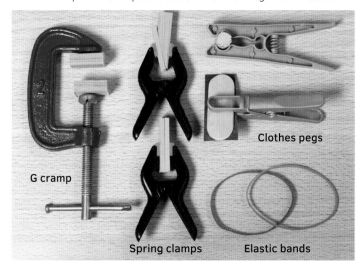

G cramp

Clothes pegs

Spring clamps

Elastic bands

Plastic spring clamps

The smallest size are ideal to hold items while glue is setting. The orange 'jaws' at each end pivot, enabling items to be clamped at an angle.

Razor saw

A small saw that is ideal for making fine cuts in wood, plastic and soft metals.

Right-angled gluing jig

A frame, often homemade, with two fixed sides set at right angles to ensure that the object is held square while the glue dries. Toy building blocks are a good alternative to a homemade jig.

Sandpaper

Also known as abrasive paper and used for smoothing wood available in a range of grades. Fine-grade sandpaper is the most commonly used in dolls' house construction.

RIGHT Toy building blocks are a good alternative to a homemade jig.

ABOVE A small general woodworking kit will come in very handy and can be built up gradually.

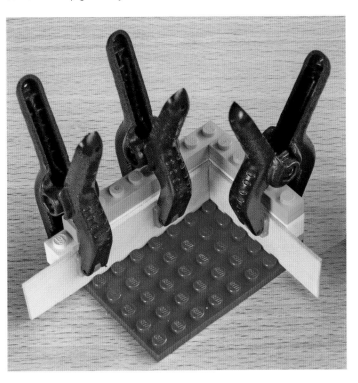

GLUES AND TAPES

Clear adhesive
A solvent-based glue useful for plastics and other non-porous materials.

Double-sided foam tape
A useful tape for simple upholstery and where you want to add some depth between layers.

Double-sided sticky tape
Ideal for paper and card as it does not moisten the surface and cause it to crinkle like glue.

Epoxy resin
A two part compound, where you mix a little glue with an equal amount of hardener, apply and leave to harden chemically.

Fabric glue
Useful when marking out material, it sticks the threads together so the fabric does not fray.

Glue gun
A gun that heats a stick of glue. Depressing the trigger forces out the molten glue. Use for behind the scenes as it can be messy, exuding more than is required. Stays hot after application so take care.

Masking tape
A strong tape that is adhesive on one side that is useful for marking out areas or holding things temporarily while they dry.

PVA glue (polyvinyl acetate)
A general purpose white glue that dries clear. It works on porous materials such as wood, card and mountboard.

Superglue (cyanoacrylate)
A strong, non-runny glue, which bonds instantly. You must resist the temptation to reposition parts once sandwiched together, as this breaks the bond.

Wallpaper border adhesive
Much thicker than PVA, making it easier to spread evenly, wallpaper border adhesive can be used for gluing paper, card, mountboard and so on.

MATERIALS

Artist's chalks, pastels and eyeshadows
Various shades can be used to weather items, or build up different shades of colour on food made from polymer clay.

Baby powder
Fine talcum powder, such as baby powder, can be used to create a layer of dust.

Beads
Beads are commonly used for details and to make items such as perfume bottles. It is worth building up a collection of beads in various sizes, shapes and colours.

Cocktail sticks
Useful for applying superglue. They can also be used as a substitute for small items of dowel, or when painted turned into miniature pencils and other items.

Fabric
Cotton is much more forgiving than silk and easier to work with. Hems can be glued rather than sewn. But silk has a wonderful lustre and hangs better once you spend the extra time to battle its slipperiness.

Jewellery findings
Metal components for jewellery making, such as bead caps and jump rings.

MDF
MDF is a manufactured material created from hardwood and softwood fibres compacted with resin. It is generally very easy to work with, but produces a lot of dust when cut.

Paints

You will need a range of paints depending on the job you are tackling. Emulsion is good for interior and exterior walls, acrylic for details and enamel paints for small metallic items.

Plywood

This is made from thin sheets of wood veneer sandwiched together so that the grain direction alternates with each layer to prevent warping and twisting.

Polymer clay

A modelling clay that can be baked in domestic ovens to make items solid and long lasting. It is commonly used to make food and modern household appliances like toasters and mixers.

Shoe polish

Brown polish works particularly well for ageing and staining small pieces of wood.

Varnish

A water-based or oil-based medium that gives a shiny finish when dry. (Clear nail-varnish can be used as an alternative). Available also in satin and matt for duller finishes.

Wire

Jewellery-making wire and paper cover wire are ideal for use in making plants and flowers.

Wood stain

Available as either a water-based or oil-based preparation to colour wood.

3D PRINTING RESOURCES

If you are tempted to give 3D printing a try, there are lots of tools and resources available online to help you. Here are just a few:

Design packages

Sketchup; Blender; Design Spark Mechanical; Tinkercad; OpenSCAD; 3DTin; Onshape; Shapesmith; Autodesk 123Design; Cheetah 3D

Design libraries

www.thingiverse.com
www.youmagine.com
3dwarehouse.sketchup.com
sketchfab.com
Many of the objects the British Museum has made public are on Sketchfab.

Checking software

Autodesk Netfabb

Slicing software

Cura; Repetier Host; Slic3r

Printer manufacturers

Ultimaker; MakerBot; Printrbot; Da Vinci; UP; XYZprinting; Dremel

Print shops

4D Model Shop; Blueprint Modelshop; 3DPRINTUK; Shapeways

Online resources

www.hongkiat.com/blog/60-excellent-free-3d-model-websites

Acknowledgements

Thank you to the following miniaturists, whose work has been featured in this book:

Jodi Sophia Anderson; Sophie Anderson; Liza Antrim; Gale Bantock; Katina Beale; Christiane Berridge; Carol Black; Christine Bloxham; Bromley Craft Products; Chris Brooking, Firecraft Miniatures; Terry Brown; Tee Bylo; Aidan Campbell; Julie Campbell; Linda Carswell; Roz Clackett; Peggy Connolly; Sue Cook; Diane Cooper; Nell Corkin; Carol Cranmer; John Cutts; Joelle Dade; Liz Davis; Gerry de Cave; Giac Dell'accio; Elaine Diehl; Heather Drinkwater; Peter Dryden; Patrick Duclou; Caroline Dupuis; Ruth Flewelling Lesbirel; Karin Foster; Adam Fray and Lauren Hicks; Christine-Léa Frisoni; Dolph Gotelli; Stan Gregg; Amy Gross; Caroline Hamilton; Kristine Hanna, Paperdollminiatures.com; Angela Hartnall; Claudia Hill-Sparks; John Hodgson/Hever Castle; Amanda Hope; Megan Hornbecker; Ron Hubble; Tove Jansson; Claude Joachim; Mel Jones; Grazhina Kayhart; Sue Kendall, Molly Sue Miniatures; Jennifer Kennedy Halter; Beate Klotz; Carol Kubrican, True2Scale Miniatures; Annemarie Kwikkel; Eileen Lang; Karon Lesley; Heather Macdonald; Maria Malmström; Charles Matton; Emma Mawston; Irene McCulloch; Caroline McFarlane-Watts; Jo Medvenics; Emma Metcalf; Jacky Miles; Miniature Mansions; Kevin Mulvaney and Susie Rogers; Nature's Soul Miniatures; Deborah Newell; Amy Nikolai; Jean Nisbett; Robert Off; Brae Oktober; Jennifer Osmond Hatt; Josephine Parnell; Pendon Museum; Petite Properties; Rik Pierce; Puppenhausmuseum; Arabella Ramsay; Sara Read; Ingeborg Riesser; Vera Rijgersberg, Montheron; Tom Roberts; Maggie Rudy; Marion Russek; Kim Saulter; Karina Schaapman; Joanne Schmidt; Mel Sebastian, Mad Missy Minis; Joelle Sheard-Patrick; Jan Simpson Gilham; Elizabeth Slinn; Mercedes Spencer; Renate Stettler; Kathleen Stewart; Susan Stobart; Anna-Maria Sviatko; Ann Taylor; The Thorne Rooms; Pat and Noel Thomas; Jessica Townsend Melton; Peter Tucker; Sean Valentine; Josje Veenenbos; Pam Veiler; Emma Waddell; Geoffrey Walkley; Lyn Waters and Heather Hooper; Margaret Watson; Matthew Weston; Wildwood Dollhouses; Nevile Wilkinson; Richard Wilson.

Thank you to the following individuals whose contributions to *The Dolls' House Magazine* have been fundamental to the creation of this book:

Lynn Allingham; Beryl Armstrong; Anthony Bailey; Karen Bamford; Martha Bamford; Louise Bardwell; Christiane Berridge; Beth Blight; John Bristow; Daniel Brookbank; Natalie Clegg; Sue Cook; John Cutts; Catherine Davies; Katy Evans; Ruth Flewelling Lesbirel; Janet Granger; Janet Harmsworth; John Harris; Angela Hartnall; Katie Holloway; Beate Klotz; Jane Laverick; Kelly Murdie; Wanna Newman; Jean Nisbett; John Payne; Frances Powell; Lesley Rands.

Index

A

To order a book, or to request a catalogue, contact:

GMC Publications Ltd

Castle Place, 166 High Street, Lewes, East Sussex

BN7 1XU, United Kingdom

Tel: +44 (0)1273 488005

www.gmcbooks.com